A Passport for Crockpot Cooking

Slow Cooker Recipes for the New American Table

Kevin M. Cordeiro

Published in 2017 by Downton Publishing
www.downtonpublishing.com

ISBN: 0692870954
ISBN-13: 978-0692870952

Table of Contents

Introduction

Dear Reader, thank you for purchasing A Passport for Crockpot Cooking.

In this cookbook, I share with you my favorite recipes from around the world. Recipes from diverse cultures passed down from generation to generation.

Join me as I cook my way around America and try many different foods. I believe in mastering one recipe and then making variations. Most of the recipes in this book are quick and easy to prepare, however if texture and taste were compromised there's an added step is in the beginning or end. I hope you love these recipes as much as I do.

Enjoy!
Sincerely,
Kevin M. Cordeiro

United States – The Great Melting Pot

This map shows the top 14 largest population of "New America" foods available in the Unites States today. As you can see The United States is quite the melting pot of diverse cultures.

Foods of the world aren't just sauces and condiments, nor are they Asian, Italian, and Mexican. Manufacturers are striving to satisfy demand with more variety, spice, and bold flavors. Specialty and international food aisles are increasing in supermarkets as consumers want more interesting fare.

United States international foods are more popular now because international travel, immigration and global trade have skyrocketed, driving great interest in ethnic cuisine. United States retail sales of international foods totaled $11 billion in 2013, says statista.com. This will generate more than $12.5 billion by 2018. Most sales are by Mexican/Hispanic foods with $1.6 billion, followed by products with an Asian/Indian heritage.

According to research by the National Restaurant Association., 88 percent of American consumers eat at least one international food item per month, while 17 percent eat seven or more. One-third of consumers tried a new specialty cuisine in the past year. In fact, non-traditional cuisines have been on the rise in the past decade.

There is soaring growth in authentic flavor profiles and bold flavors in various Asian foods including Thai, Indian and Japanese. Asian flavors will continue to abound as familiar ingredients such as wasabi, ginger and soy give way to cardamom, five-spice, fish sauce and lime. Consumers have become much more adventurous in food choices, with increasing demand for Vietnam's goi con and pho. Asian flavor profiles focus on achieving a balance of sweet, sour, salty, umami and spicy, often in the same dish.

Food processors are finding sorts of ways to meet consumer wants for bold flavors while keeping healthfulness in mind. You will see spicy Asian condiment gochujang added on meat, seafood, and poultry and in sauces, marinades, and rubs. According to the annual flavor predictions from McCormick & Co. Sambal sauce from Indonesia, made with chilies, rice vinegar and garlic, is another spicy find the Hunt Valley, Md. company has identified as an upcoming trend.

Lee Kum Kee has produced Chinese condiments and food products for years. They are now taking things a few steps further with more intense flavors. Its newest product, Sriracha Mayo, is a spicy sauce with a creamy texture that can add a kick to sandwiches, wraps, tacos or as a dipping sauce. Building off the long-standing success of Sriracha Chili Sauce, Sriracha Mayo combines traditional flavors of sriracha with the cool and creamy texture of mayo. The spicy flavor and mayonnaise smoothness give the sauce distinction when combined with other ingredients. Great as a marinade for chicken, meat, and seafood dishes.

Campbell Soup listed Thai food as one of its top food trends for 2017. Homestyle dishes found throughout Thailand, such as khao soy curry noodle soup, are hitting independent restaurants, say Campbell's network of chefs, bakers, and culinary professionals. They also see creative ramen and Vietnamese pho dishes rising in popularity. Campbell's Culinary & Baking Institute, last month, launched a new line of fresh refrigerated ramen noodles at the Winter Fancy Food show.

This year McCormick is launching 56 new consumer products inspired by McCormick's Flavor forecast trends. McCormick has been tracking the growth of 'heat,' and identifying upcoming spice flavors including chipotle, peri-peri and herissa. Look for Southeast Asian sambal sauce to take kitchens by storm.

Heat will remain on the rise, as millennials prefer spicy and exotic foods. Many spice enthusiasts have been searching for the next sriracha. According to the U.S. Census Bureau, the Hispanic population in America is projected to more than double in the next 40 years, from 55 million to an amazing 119 million. This will likely compel food companies to rethink product formulations that are more multicultural, accommodating the Latin American – not just the Mexican market – with food from more Latin cultures.

CHINESE

Mongolian Beef page 19

There are over 43,000 Chinese restaurants in the United States. This is higher than any other domestic fast food restaurants. Chinese cuisine is one of the richest and boasts the most diverse culinary tradition in the world. Chinese food is categorized by the regional area from which they originate.

Canton cuisine is from the southern area that emphasizes frying, roasting, steaming, and poaching. Shanghai cuisine is from the eastern part of China. It is delicate, sweet in flavor, and not oily or greasy.

Beijing cuisine is from the northern part of China featuring elegant dishes that are strong, spicy, and generous in using garlic.

Hunan/Szechuan cuisine is from the western part of China that uses hot, strong, and spicy flavors involving chili, peppers, spices, and herbs.

Sticky Chicken Wings

Serves 4

Ingredients:
15-20 chicken wings
⅓ cup soy sauce
⅓ cup balsamic vinegar
½ cup brown sugar
½ cup honey
¼ teaspoon ginger powder
½ teaspoon ground pepper
½ teaspoon garlic powder
½ teaspoon onion powder
2 tablespoons cornstarch

There's no hot oil and no deep frying. Cook everything in your crock pot, then quickly broil for crispness. It's just that easy. The results are unbelievably amazing. These wings are cooked perfectly, soaked in all that flavor for hours on end. And the meat literally falls off the bone!

1. In a large bowl, whisk together soy sauce, balsamic vinegar, brown sugar, honey, ginger powder, pepper, garlic powder and onion powder. Place wings into a crock pot.
2. Stir in soy sauce mixture and gently toss to combine.
3. Cover with lid and cook 3 hours on high or 6 hours on low.
4. Preheat oven to broil. Grease a baking sheet.
5. Carefully remove cooked wings from crock pot onto the baking sheet.
6. In a cup, add cornstarch with 3 tablespoons of liquid form the crock pot, stir until smooth and then mix into the crock pot.
7. Pour some sauce from crock pot all over the wings.
8. Broil for 2-3 minutes, or until caramelized and slightly charred.

General Tso Chicken Wings

Serves 4

Ingredients:
15-20 chicken wings
¼ cup soy sauce
¼ cup brown sugar
3 cloves garlic, minced
1 teaspoon dry ground ginger
½ teaspoon cayenne pepper
¼ teaspoon ground black pepper
½ teaspoon salt
1 tablespoon cornstarch
1 tablespoon sesame seeds, for garnish
1 green onion, sliced for garnish

General Tso's Chicken has been one of America's most popular Chinese takeout dishes for decades and is a Chinese-American creation. And a great one at that.
Next time you're craving General Tso's chicken, skip the takeout joint – this recipe with chicken wings will rival your favorite takeout.

1. Place chicken wings in a large slow-cooker.
2. In a large bowl, mix together soy sauce, brown sugar, garlic, ginger, cayenne pepper, salt, and black pepper. Add cornstarch and stir until mixed. Pour over chicken and mix.
3. Cover with lid and cook 3 hours on high or 6 hours on low.
4. Heat broiler. Line two baking sheets with parchment paper and pour wings onto them. Broil until crispy, 5 minutes.
5. Sprinkle with sesame seeds and green onion, serve.

Beef and Broccoli

Serves 4

Ingredients:
1 pound beef stew meat
1 bag frozen broccoli florets
1 cup beef broth or stock
¼ cup soy sauce
⅓ cup brown sugar or honey
1 teaspoon sesame oil
3 teaspoons minced garlic
¼ teaspoon dry ground ginger
2 tablespoons cornstarch
Cooked rice (optional)

This is a great recipe when you want Chinese food without having to go out. It's very easy and delicious. Substituting chicken for the beef works great too!

1. Place beef in a crock pot.
2. In a small bowl, combine broth, soy sauce, brown sugar or honey, oil, ginger, and garlic.
3. Pour over beef.
4. Cover with lid and cook 3 hours on high or 6 hours on low.
5. Add broccoli to the crock pot. Stir to combine.
6. Cover and cook an additional 1 hour on high
7. In a cup, add cornstarch with 3 tablespoons of liquid form the crock pot, stir until smooth and then mix into the crock pot.
8. Cover and cook on high for an additional 30 minutes. Serve over hot cooked rice.

Cashew Chicken

Serves 4

Ingredients:
3 boneless, skinless chicken breasts, cut into small cubes
1 teaspoon salt
½ teaspoon ground black pepper
1 tablespoons extra-virgin olive oil
2 dried hot chili peppers
2 cups bok choy (Chinese cabbage)
1 cup cashews, toasted
2 tablespoons cornstarch
¼ cup low-sodium soy sauce
2 cloves garlic, minced
2 tablespoons hoisin sauce
1 tablespoon rice wine vinegar
1 tablespoon brown sugar
1 tablespoon ketchup
1 tablespoon chili sauce
¼ teaspoon sesame oil
¼ teaspoon dry ground ginger
1 cup chicken stock

Cashew chicken is a simple Chinese-American dish that combines chicken, with cashews, in a delicious sauce. Forget takeout and cook in with Cashew Chicken. A flavorful and sweet sauce tossed with chicken and chili peppers for added heat.

1. Season the chicken with the salt and pepper.
2. Heat olive oil in a large pan or skillet over medium-high heat and cook chicken for 2-3 minutes, per side, or until browned, then transfer to slow cooker and add bok choy and peppers.
3. In a bowl, whisk together soy sauce, garlic, hoisin sauce, rice wine vinegar, brown sugar, ketchup, chili sauce, sesame oil, ginger, and chicken stock.
4. Drizzle sauce over the chicken, bok choy and pepper. Toss together to combine.
5. Cover with lid and cook 3 hours on high or 6 hours on low.
6. In a cup, add cornstarch with 3 tablespoons of liquid form the crock pot, stir until smooth and then mix into the crock pot. Mix in cashews
7. Cover and cook on high for an additional 30 minutes.

Hunan Orange Chicken

Serves 4

Ingredients:
2-pounds boneless chicken cut into bite size pieces
1 red pepper, cut into strips
1 yellow pepper, cut into strips
1 tablespoon minced garlic
½ teaspoon dry ground ginger
¼ cup sugar
1 teaspoon salt
½ teaspoon black pepper
¼ teaspoon crushed hot pepper flakes
12-ounces frozen orange juice concentrate (no pulp)
2 tablespoons cornstarch

This is a delicious citrus chicken recipe with flavors reminiscent of the orange chicken from a popular restaurant. Orange chicken is an American Chinese dish of Hunan origin. Recipe consists of chopped chicken pieces coated in a sweet orange-flavored sauce. While the dish is very popular in the United States, it is most often found as a variation of General Tso's chicken rather than the dish found in mainland China.

1. Mix together first 10 ingredients in crock pot.
2. Cover with lid and cook 3 hours on high or 6 hours on low.
3. In a cup, add cornstarch with 3 tablespoons of liquid form the crock pot, stir until smooth and then mix into the crock pot.
4. Cover and cook on high for an additional 30 minutes.

Serve chicken over precooked noodles or white rice.

Mongolian Beef

Serves 4

Ingredients:
1 ½ pound flank steak sliced very
thin (sirloin works as well)
¼ cup cornstarch
1 red pepper, sliced
1 medium onion, sliced thin
¼ teaspoon dry ground ginger
1 tablespoon minced garlic
½ cup soy sauce
½ cup water
¾ cup dark brown sugar

**Garnish - 3 medium green onions,
chopped**

This dish is served in Chinese-American restaurants. The name of this dish is somewhat misleading, as aside from the beef, none of the ingredients or the preparation methods is drawn from traditional Mongolian cuisine. The term "Mongolian" is rather meant to imply an "exotic" type of food.

1. Spray crock pot with non-stick cooking spray.
2. Place cornstarch in a bowl. Coat each piece of steak in cornstarch and place in crock pot. Discard any remaining cornstarch.
3. Add peppers and onions to crock pot over beef.
4. In a bowl combine remaining ingredients, except green onions and pour over beef and vegetables in crock pot.
5. Cover with lid and cook 3 hours on high or 6 hours on low.
Serve over cooked rice, topped with sliced green onions.

Sesame Honey Chicken

Serves 4

Ingredients:
2-pounds boneless chicken cut into bite size pieces
1 medium onion, chopped
2 teaspoons minced garlic
½ cup honey
¼ cup tomato sauce
½ cup soy sauce
½ teaspoon salt
½ teaspoon ground black pepper
2 tablespoons cornstarch
1-2 tablespoons sesame seeds

This dish is commonly found in Chinese restaurants throughout the English-speaking world. The dish is like General Tso's chicken but the taste of the Chinese-based chicken is sweet rather than spicy. This dish is popular almost solely in the United States.

1. Place chicken and onion in a crock pot.
2. In a small bowl, combine garlic, honey, tomato sauce, soy sauce, salt and black pepper and pour over chicken.
3. Cover with lid and cook 4 hours on high or 8 hours on low.
4. In a cup, add cornstarch with 3 tablespoons of liquid form the crock pot, stir until smooth and then mix into the crock pot.
5. Cover and cook on high for an additional 30 minutes.
6. Serve over hot cooked rice garnish with sesame seeds.

Shanghai Shrimp

Serves 4

Ingredients:
¼ cup ketchup
2 tablespoons rice wine vinegar or red wine vinegar
1 tablespoon soy sauce
1 tablespoon dry sherry wine
2 tablespoons sugar
¼ teaspoon dry ground ginger
3 scallions cut into 2 inch pieces
½ teaspoon salt
¼ teaspoon black pepper
1 pound large raw shrimp, peeled, deveined and tail shells removed.

Shanghai cuisine is epitomized using alcohol, fish, crab, or chicken and is "drunken" with spirits. Sugar is also very common in Shanghai cuisine, especially when used in combination with soy sauce. The most notable dish of this type of cooking is "sweet and sour shrimp".

1. Add all ingredients to crock pot EXCEPT shrimp.
2. Cover with lid and cook 2 hours on high or 4 hours on low.
3. Mix in shrimp and cook an additional hour on high.

Moo Goo Gai Pan

Serves 4

Ingredients:
3 boneless chicken breasts, cut into bite size pieces
1 teaspoon fresh grated ginger
1 teaspoon salt
½ teaspoon white pepper
2 teaspoons minced garlic
1 ½ cups chicken stock
½ pound sliced mushrooms
¼ pound snow peas
1 (8 ounce) cans water chestnuts, drained
1 (8 ounce) cans bamboo shoots, drained
1 carrot (thin sliced)
2 tablespoons cornstarch

Cooked white rice

There's no hot oil and no deep frying. Cook everything in your crock pot, then quickly broil for crispness. It's just that easy. The results are unbelievably amazing. These wings are cooked perfectly, soaked in all that flavor for hours on end. And the meat literally falls off the bone!

1. Add and mix all ingredients to crock pot EXCEPT cornstarch.
2. Cover with lid and cook 3 hours on high or 4 hours on low.
3. In a cup, add cornstarch with 3 tablespoons of liquid form the crock pot, stir until smooth and then mix into the crock pot.
4. Serve over cooked white rice.

Kung Pao Chicken

Serves 4

Ingredients:
3 boneless chicken breasts, cut into
1-inch cubes
1 red pepper, chopped into 1-inch
cubes
1 green pepper, chopped into 1-inch
cubes
6 tablespoons soy sauce
2 tablespoons hoisin sauce
2 tablespoons balsamic vinegar
4 tablespoons brown sugar
2 teaspoons minced garlic
½ teaspoon crushed red pepper
flakes
2 teaspoons Sriracha sauce or 8 red
hot dried chili peppers
2 tablespoons corn starch
½ cup peanuts

This highly addictive chicken continues to be one of the most popular Chinese dishes in America as the succulent, complex sauce of salty, sweet, sour, and spicy flavors is hard to pass up.

1. Add and mix all ingredients in your crock pot EXCEPT corn starch and peanuts.
2. Cover with lid and cook 3 hours on high or 6 hours on low.
3. In a cup, add cornstarch with 3 tablespoons of liquid form the crock pot, stir until smooth and then mix into the crock pot. Mix in peanuts.

Szechuan Green Beans & Mushrooms

Serves 4

Ingredients:
1 pound fresh green beans, ends trimmed
7-ounces shiitake mushrooms, stems removed and sliced
3 tablespoons soy sauce
1 can chicken broth
1 ½ tablespoons sherry wine
½ teaspoon sesame oil
1 teaspoons sugar
½ teaspoon cornstarch
¼ teaspoon crushed red hot pepper flakes
¼ teaspoon dry mustard
1 tablespoon minced garlic
1 tablespoon grated fresh ginger

This restaurant style Szechuan green beans is a perfect combination of vegetables, with savory and slightly spicy taste. This is a delicious Chinese side dish.

1. Add chicken broth in your crock pot.
2. Add green beans and shiitake mushrooms.
3. Blend soy sauce, chicken broth, sherry, sesame oil, sugar, cornstarch, hot pepper flakes, dry mustard, garlic, and ginger.
4. Pour over green beans and mushrooms.
5. Cover with lid and cook 3 hours on high or 6 hours on low.

DOMINICAN

Pollo Guisado (Chicken Stew) page 28

Dominican cuisine is predominantly made up of a combination of Spanish, indigenous Taíno, and African influences. Many Middle-Eastern dishes have been adopted into Dominican cuisine, such as the "Quipe" that comes from the Lebanese kibbeh. Dominican cuisine resembles that of other countries in Latin America, those of the nearby islands of Puerto Rico and Cuba, most of all, though the dish names differ sometimes.

A traditional breakfast would consist of mangú, fried eggs, fried salami, fried cheese and sometimes avocado. This is called "Los Tres Golpes" or "The Three Hits". As in Spain, the largest, most important meal of the day is lunch. Its most typical form, nicknamed La Bandera ("The Flag"), consists of rice, red beans, and meat (beef, chicken, pork, or fish), sometimes accompanied by a side of salad.

Alitas Barbecue (Chicken Wings)

Serves 4

Ingredients:
15-24 chicken wings

BBQ Sauce:
1 cup water
4 tablespoons melted butter
1 shot glass of whiskey
½ cup tomato sauce
1 tablespoon orange juice
1 tablespoon lemon juice
⅓ cup honey
⅓ cup of your favorite salsa
1 teaspoon salt
¼ teaspoon ground black pepper
2 tablespoons dark brown sugar

A good barbecue sauce can add life to a lot of your favorite dishes. Making your own BBQ sauce is very easy and the results are so tasty, you may never use the bottled sauce again. As with all the good things in life, there are several ways to make a delicious sauce. This is another great Dominican recipe for chicken wings.

1. Place Chicken wings in crock pot.
2. Combine all sauce ingredients and blend together well and pour over chicken wings, mix in.
3. Cover with lid and cook 3 hours on high or 6 hours on low.
4. Remove wings carefully to a greased cookie sheet, as the wings will be very tender.
5. Baste wings with a little more sauce from crock pot.
6. Broil in oven for 5-10 minutes and baste wings again.

Res Guisada (Braised Beef Stew)

Serves 4

Ingredients:
1 pound of beef (round or skirt) cut into small pieces.
2 tablespoons of oil (corn, canola, or peanut)
1 teaspoon of salt
¼ teaspoon ground black pepper
1 medium potato, diced
1 carrot, diced
1 tablespoon lime juice
A pinch of dried oregano
1 ½ cups of beef broth
½ red onion cut into slices
1 tomato, chopped
1 bell pepper, chopped
1 tablespoon minced garlic
1 cup of tomato sauce

I must say that this recipe is not only a staple dish in Dominican culture, but it is also by far one of my favorites. The beef always comes out tender, succulent and so flavorful! You need to brown the meat first, but worth every second, trust me!

1. In a pan heat the oil over medium heat.
2. Season beef with salt and pepper. Add the beef and brown on both sides.
3. Add browned beef to your crock pot with all the juices from the pan.
4. Mix all other ingredients with the beef in crock pot.
5. Cover with lid and cook 3 hours on high or 6 hours on low.

Pollo Guisado (Chicken Stew)

Serves 4

Ingredients:
6 boneless chicken thighs
2 tablespoons tomato paste
½ cup water
1 tablespoon sugar
1 tablespoon olive oil
¼ cups white vinegar
1 package of Goya sazon
1 tablespoon garlic, minced
¼ teaspoon dried oregano
¼ cup Goya Mojo criollo
(marinade)
1 teaspoon Goya Adobo all-
purpose seasoning
¼ teaspoons ground black
pepper
¼ cup tomato sauce
1 onion, sliced
½ red bell peppers, sliced
3 tablespoon green olives,
sliced

This delicious one-pot chicken stew is a weekly staple in many Dominican homes. It's a simple recipe that comes together in no time. Mix everything together in a slow cooker, cover and cook. It's really that simple! This dish alongside rice and beans makes up a patriotic lunch called "la bandera" otherwise known as the Dominican flag.

1. Mix and dissolve tomato paste in water.
2. Mix all ingredients in crock pot EXCEPT green olives.
3. Cover with lid and cook 4 hours on high or 8 hours on low.

Garnish with green olives

Pernil (Pork Shoulder)

Serves 6

Ingredients:
1 pork shoulder, 4 to 7 pounds
1 cup water
½ cup red wine
2 tablespoons olive oil
1 tablespoon minced garlic
1 large onion, chopped
½ teaspoon dried oregano
¼ teaspoon dried thyme
1 tablespoon ground cumin
1 teaspoon chili powder
1 tablespoon kosher salt
2 teaspoons freshly ground
black pepper

This classic Puerto Rican recipe for roast pork makes a festive centerpiece for a Memorial Day feast, a delicious welcome to summer. The process is beyond easy and incredibly impressive, it feeds as many people as a medium-size ham, and the flavor is unbelievable.

1. Add water and wine to crock pot.
2. Pulse garlic, onion, oregano, thyme, cumin, chili, salt and pepper together in a food processor, adding oil in a drizzle and scraping down sides as necessary, until mixture is pasty. (Alternatively, mash ingredients in a mortar and pestle.)
3. Using a knife make small slits across the skin of the pork.
4. Rub this mixture well into pork, getting it into every nook and cranny and add pork to your crock pot.
5. Cover with lid and cook 5 hours on high or 10 hours on low.

Costillas de Cerdo (Barbecue Pork Ribs)

Serves 4

Ingredients:
4 pounds of pork ribs
1 cup beef broth

BBQ Sauce:
2 tablespoons brown sugar
2 tablespoons Worcestershire sauce
1 tablespoon vinegar
3 drops of tabasco sauce
1 teaspoon garlic powder
¼ teaspoon powdered mustard
¼ teaspoon salt
½ cup ketchup

Chivo guisado is another favorite stew present in many special celebrations in the Dominican Republic. This is a recipe from the Northwest of the Dominican Republic where goats are said to feed on wild oregano. A popular area where you can get fresh goat meat by the pound or whole. This is a spicy stew of tender and flavorful goat meat.

1. Add broth and ribs to your crock pot.
2. It a bowl mix all BBQ sauce ingredients together. Reserve a ¼ cup of this sauce for later.
3. Pour remaining sauce over pork ribs.
4. Cover with lid and cook 3 hours on high or 6 hours on low.

Baste ribs before serving with reserved BBQ sauce.

FILIPINO

Pininyahang Manok sa Gata (Chicken with Pineapple) page 35

Filipino cuisine centers on the combination of sweet, sour, and salty, although in Bicol, and among Muslim Filipinos, spicy is the base of cooking flavor. Philippine cuisine comes in a pairing of something sweet with something salty, and results in a surprisingly pleasing combination. Vinegar is a common ingredient. Adobo is popular not solely for its simplicity and ease of preparation, but also for its ability to be stored for days without spoiling, and even improve in flavor with a day or two of storage.

Cooking and eating in the Philippines has traditionally been an informal and communal affair centered around the family kitchen. Filipinos traditionally eat three main meals a day, plus an afternoon snack. Food tends to be served all at once and not in courses. Unlike many of their Asian counterpart's Filipinos do not eat with chopsticks. Due to Western influence, food is often eaten using flatware—forks, knives, spoons—but the primary pairing of utensils used at a Filipino dining table is that of spoon and fork, not knife and fork.

Sinigang na Baboy (Pork Soup)

Serves 4

Ingredients:
1 pound pork ribs, cut into
individual ribs
1 small onion, cut into wedges
1 teaspoon salt
½ teaspoon ground black pepper
1 (½ inch) piece fresh ginger,
diced
1 tablespoon fish sauce
2 plum tomatoes, cut into ½ inch
slices
5 cups water
1 (1.41 ounce) package tamarind
soup mix
½ pound fresh green beans, tips
removed

1 green onion sliced for garnish

Sinigang na Baboy, is a traditional Filipino soup dish known
for its sour flavor. By tradition, the souring ingredient of this
dish comes from a tamarind fruit. If there is one dish you
could eat every day, it would be sinigang. The sentiment is
common among Filipinos, whose mouths pucker in
anticipation of the refreshing sour soup. Pork soured with
tamarind is one of the most popular sinigang combinations.

1. Mix all ingredients in crock pot.
2. Cover with lid and cook 4 hours on high or 8 hours on
low.
3. Garnish with green onion

Beef Mami (Beef Noodle Soup)

Serves 4

Ingredients:
1 pound beef brisket, sliced
6-star anise seeds
3 beef bouillon cubes
5 cups water
1 teaspoons salt
½ teaspoon ground black pepper
1 tablespoon minced garlic
1 medium sized onion, minced
1 cup Chinese cabbage, chopped
¼ cup green onions, chopped
4 hard-boiled eggs
14 ounces egg noodles, cooked

If you grew up eating beef mami or if you are looking to try something different here is a flavorful Filipino beef dish. Filipino cuisine is inspired by Polynesian, Spanish, Chinese, and American cooking and has transformed into its own unique style and flavors. This is a delicious Filipino meat and noodle dish that is filling and flavorful.

1. Add all ingredients to your crock pot EXCEPT green onions, hard boiled eggs, and egg noodles.
2. Cover with lid and cook 3 hours on high or 6 hours on low.

Serve over cooked noodles.
Garnish each bowl with 1 hard-boiled egg sliced in half with green onion.

Giniling Guisado (Ground Beef Stew)

Serves 4

Ingredients:
1 pound of ground beef
1 large potato, diced
1 small onion, diced
1 carrot, diced
½ green bell pepper, diced
½ red bell pepper, diced
1 cup frozen peas
2 teaspoons minced garlic
3 tablespoons of soy sauce
1 tablespoon fish sauce
2 tablespoons ketchup
1 teaspoon salt
½ teaspoon ground black pepper
1 cup tomato sauce
½ cup water

Giniling Guisado is made with ground pork or ground beef depending on who's cooking, so you are free to use either or a mix of the two. The flavors in this dish are robust and overall, it's one of my favorite Filipino dishes. Giniling is a Tagalog word for ground meat and in Philippine cuisine refers to a dish made of ground pork, beef, or chicken. It is best served with hot white rice.

1. Brown ground beef, drain and add to crockpot.
2. Add all other ingredients and mix well.
3. Cover with lid and cook 4 hours on high or 8 hours on low.

Pininyahang Manok sa Gata (Chicken with Pineapple)

Serves 4

Ingredients:
1 ½ lbs. boneless chicken, cut into bite size pieces
1 (14 oz.) can pineapple chunks with juice
1 small red bell pepper, sliced
1 small green bell pepper, sliced
1 cup coconut milk
1 ½ tablespoons fish sauce
2 small carrots, sliced
1 small onion, diced
1 medium plum tomato, diced
1 teaspoon minced garlic
¼ teaspoon ground black pepper
½ teaspoon dry crushed red hot pepper flakes
½ teaspoon dry ground ginger

Pininyahang Manok sa Gata is cooked in coconut milk is the perfect Filipino dish that you can prepare for lunch during the weekend or anytime of the week. This dish is delicious and so colorful that it satisfies both your eyes and taste buds. Because of being a rich and tasty dish, it is great over steamed rice.

1. Marinate the chicken in the pineapple juice with the canned pineapple chunks for 1 to 2 hours.
2. Add the marinated chicken, pineapple chucks and the juice to your crock pot.
3. Mix in all the other ingredients.
4. Cover with lid and cook 4 hours on high or 8 hours on low.

Pork Adobo

Serves 6

Ingredients:
**2-pound pork tenderloin,
cut up into bite size pieces**
1 tablespoon minced garlic
1 small onion, chopped
1 cup water
¼ cup vinegar
4 bay leaves
**¼ teaspoons ground black
pepper or whole pepper corn**
4 tablespoons brown sugar
¼ cup soy sauce
2 tablespoons oyster sauce

Pork Adobo is pork cooked in soy sauce, vinegar, and garlic. This is considered by many as the Philippine's national dish because of its popularity, and ease in preparation. Adobo is not only limited to pork and chicken, other meats or seafood, such as squid, goat meat, veal, beef, and shrimp can also be cooked this way. This pork adobo recipe is one of the easiest and best that you will find.

1. Add all ingredients to your crock pot.
2. Cover with lid and cook 3 hours on high or 6 hours on low.

Chicken Afritada

Serves 4

Ingredients:
1 pound boneless chicken, cut
into serving pieces
1 large potato, quartered
1 large carrot, sliced
1 large bell pepper, sliced
1 cup green peas
1 cup tomato sauce
1 tablespoon minced garlic
4 hot dogs, sliced
1 medium onion, diced
1 ¼ cups chicken broth
2 bay leaves
1 teaspoon sugar
1 teaspoon salt
½ teaspoon ground black pepper

This Chicken Afritada recipe has slices of chicken cooked in tomato sauce along with onions, peppers, carrots and hot dogs. Try this awesome dish.

1. Add all ingredients to your crock pot.
2. Cover with lid and cook 3 hours on high or 6 hours on low.

Pork Menudo

Serves 4

Ingredients:
1 ½ pounds boneless pork
4 hot dogs, sliced
1 large potato, peeled and diced
1 medium carrot, cubed
1 teaspoon salt
½ teaspoon ground black pepper
½ cup soy sauce
½ teaspoon lemon juice
1 onion, chopped
1 tablespoon minced garlic
1 teaspoon sugar
1 cup tomato sauce
1 cup water
2 bay leaves

In California, menudo usually means a spicy Mexican soup made with chunks of tripe in a chili-infused broth. The recipe we have here, however, is the Filipino menudo. This is a colorful stew of pork, potatoes, carrots, and hot dogs in a thick tomato sauce. This recipe is simple and delicious.

1. Add all ingredients to your crock pot.
2. Cover with lid and cook 3 hours on high or 6 hours on low.

FRENCH

Cassoulet (Meat and Bean Stew) page 44

In the 14th century, a court chef known as "Taillevent", wrote Le Viandier, one of the earliest recipe collections of medieval France. During that time, Italian cuisine heavily influenced French cuisine. In the 17th century, chefs François Pierre La Varenne and Marie-Antoine Carême spearheaded movements that shifted French cooking away from its foreign influences and developed France's own indigenous style. Cheese and wine are a major part of the cuisine.

French cuisine consists of the cooking traditions and practices from France. The French do that so well; they can really layer flavors." In the soup-, stew-, and sauce-heavy cuisine, dishes often start with a base of mirepoix, a combination of diced celery, onions, carrots, and garlic.

A legendary French chef once said this duck and beans stew was the god of southwestern French food. He was wrong. Cassoulet is the god of ALL FOODS. Nothing — and I mean NOTHING — can match the comfort brought to you by a good cassoulet. It is the most heartwarming and delicious dish there is. Cassoulet is a rich, slow-cooked casserole originating in the south of France, containing meat, pork skin and white beans.

Onion Soup

Serves 6

Ingredients:
3-pounds onions, sliced
¼ cup sherry wine
2 tablespoon butter
6 cups beef stock
½ teaspoon Worcestershire sauce
1 bay leaf
A pinch of dried thyme
½ teaspoon salt
¼ teaspoon pepper

Garnish:
Crusty bread
Grated parmesan cheese
Shredded gruyere cheese

Is there anything more comforting on a chilly day than a hot bowl of French onion soup? Especially with a thick slice of toasted bread loaded with melty Gruyere cheese and lots of onions. And if you don't have ovenproof bowls or ramekins for the soup, don't worry—you can just top your soup with melty cheese toasts.

1. Add all ingredients to your crock pot.
2. Cover with lid and cook 4 hours on high or 8 hours on low.
3. Remove bay leaf
4. Add soup to ovenproof serving bowls and add garnish.
5. Broil in your oven till cheese is melted.

French Dip

Serves 8

Ingredients:
3-pound boneless beef rump or chuck roast, fat trimmed
½ cup red wine
1 can (10½ ounce) condensed French onion soup, undiluted
1 can (10½ ounce) condensed beef consommé, undiluted
1 can (10½ ounce) condensed beef broth, undiluted
1 teaspoon beef bouillon granules
Soft butter
8 French rolls

These French dip sandwiches are melt in your mouth tender and bursting with wonderful taste. A casual dining delight. It's also the perfect winter weather food, football party food, comforting food. Or, most importantly, you need something simple to throw together for dinner.

1. Add all ingredients to your crock pot EXCEPT butter and rolls.
2. Cover with lid and cook 4 hours on high or 8 hours on low.
3. Split French rolls, and spread with butter. Bake rolls for 10 minutes, or until heated through.
4. Slice the meat, and place on the rolls.

Serve with the juices from the crock pot for dipping.
Add cheese (optional)

Boeuf Bourguignon (Beef Burgundy)

Serves 6

Ingredients:
**2-pound boneless beef chuck, cut
into 1 inch cubes**
2 tablespoons olive oil
¼ cup flour
½ teaspoon salt
½ teaspoon pepper
1 onion, sliced
4 carrots, peeled and sliced
8 oz. package mushrooms, sliced
1 tablespoon minced garlic
2 bay leaves
1 cup red wine
½ cup beef broth

I wanted my boeuf bourguignon recipe to have tender braised beef in a silky, rich sauce with bold red wine flavor but without all the work that the classic recipe requires. I braised the meat over the stove first before adding the meat to my crock pot.

1. Combine the flour, salt, and black pepper.
2. Dredge the beef cubes in the flour mixture.
3. Heat the olive oil in a skillet over medium heat.
4. Brown the meat.
5. Place the beef and remaining ingredients into the crock pot, mix thoroughly.
6. Cover with lid and cook 3 hours on high or 6 hours on low.

Enchaud Perigordine (Apple Pork Loin)

Serves 8

Ingredients:
4-pound pork loin roast, bone-in
3 tablespoons olive oil
1 teaspoon salt
½ teaspoon ground black pepper
2 granny smith apples (peeled, cored, and diced)
2 cups of chicken broth
2 tablespoons minced garlic
1 onion, sliced
2 tablespoons butter
1 teaspoon Dijon mustard
1 teaspoon honey
½ cup white wine
½ cup red wine

Enchaud Perigordine is a fancy name for what's a relatively simple French dish. The pork tenderloin is juicy, moist and is full of flavor. That's exactly what you'll get with this easy pork tenderloin recipe. The roast turns out incredibly moist and delicious, but it's also slow cooked with apples and onions.

1. Sprinkle all sides of the pork loin with salt and pepper.
2. Heat olive oil on medium high heat.
3. Brown meat on all sides and add to your crock pot. Be sure to add all the drippings from the pan to your crock pot.
4. Add all other ingredients to your crock pot.
5. Cover with lid and cook 4 hours on high or 8 hours on low.

Cassoulet (Meat and Bean Stew)

Serves 4

Ingredients:
4 bone-in, skin-on chicken thighs
½ pound bacon, cut crosswise into ½ inch strips
2-3 links garlic pork sausage, sliced
1 teaspoon salt
½ teaspoon ground black pepper
1 large onion, chopped
3 celery stalks, chopped
2 carrots, peeled and chopped
2 tablespoon minced garlic
¼ cup tomato paste
½ cup white wine
1 can Northern white beans (15.5 oz)
1 bay leaf
A pinch of dried thyme
½ cup chicken stock

Garnish:
Panko bread crumbs
Dried parsley

Beloved by generations of French cooks, cassoulet is a rustic, slow-cooked dish made with white beans and a lavish assortment of meats, from chicken, duck confit to sausages and succulent cuts of pork, lamb, or poultry. Here, is an adaptation to simplify the dish for home cooks, utilizing your slow cooker.

1. In a pan, over medium heat, add the bacon and cook till bacon is crisp.
2. Remove the bacon to a plate and cover.
3. Raise the heat to medium-high and add the chicken to the bacon fat, skin side down. Brown the chicken on both sides and then remove chicken to your crock pot. Be sure to add all the drippings from the pan to your crock pot.
4. Add all other ingredients, including the cooked bacon, to your crock pot, EXCEPT garnish.
5. Cover with lid and cook 4 hours on high or 8 hours on low.

Sprinkle garnish on top of each serving dish.

Chicken Provencal

Serves 4

Ingredients:
6 boneless skinless chicken thighs
1 small onion, finely chopped
1 teaspoon dried basil
½ teaspoon dried tarragon
¼ teaspoon dried oregano
⅛ teaspoon dried thyme
1 teaspoon salt
½ teaspoon pepper
1 tablespoon minced garlic
Lemon zest from ½ a lemon
⅓ cup Kalamata olives, quartered
½ cup dry white wine
½ cup chicken stock
2 cups crushed tomatoes

The best chicken Provençal recipe would produce a dish with meltingly tender, moist, and flavorful chicken, napped in an aromatic, garlicky tomato sauce that could be mopped up with a thick slice of French crusty bread. To achieve this ideal, I used chicken thighs for their tender texture and crushed tomatoes. I seasoned the dish with dried herbs, as well as with grated lemon zest and Kalamata olives, for a chicken Provençal recipe you will be proud of.

1. Spray crock pot with non-stick cooking spray.
2. Add chicken thighs and onions to crockpot. Sprinkle with basil, tarragon, oregano, thyme, salt, and pepper.
3. Mix together garlic, lemon zest, olives, wine, chicken stock and tomatoes. Pour over chicken.
4. Cover with lid and cook 3 hours on high or 6 hours on low.

Country Chicken

Serves 4

Ingredients:
1 medium onion, chopped
2 cups baby carrots
4 celery ribs, sliced
4 red skin potatoes, quartered
4 boneless chicken breasts, cut in half
1 teaspoon dried tarragon
¼ teaspoon dried thyme
1 teaspoon salt
½ teaspoon ground black pepper
1 (10 ¾ ounce) can condensed cream of chicken soup
1 envelope dry onion soup mix
⅓ cup white wine
½ cup chicken broth

There is nothing better in this world than coming home to an awesome, flavor-packed supper that cooked up without you. Having a crock pot is like having a little automated chef that does all the cooking for you. Enjoy this delicious chicken dish.

1. Place onion, carrots, celery, and potatoes in crock pot.
2. Arrange chicken over vegetables. Sprinkle with tarragon, thyme, salt, and pepper.
3. Pour cream of chicken soup over chicken.
4. Sprinkle with dry onion soup mix and then pour in white wine and chicken broth.
5. Cover with lid and cook 3 hours on high or 6 hours on low.

Chicken Pot Pie

Serves 6

Ingredients:
2 pounds boneless, skinless chicken breast
2 cans (10.75 oz. each) cream of chicken soup
1 package Lipton onion soup mix
2 cups frozen mixed vegetables
2 potatoes, peeled and cut up into bite size pieces
1 ½ cups chicken broth
½ teaspoon dried tarragon
2 tablespoons butter
1 package of grands flaky layers biscuits dough like, Pillsbury

Thursday night is chicken pot pie night...or at least at the many family restaurants in the French Quarter of New Orleans. This is a classic chicken pot pie. It has some French herbs, like tarragon, and Pillsbury grands flaky layers biscuits to make the crust easy!

1. Spray crock pot with non-stick cooking spray.
2. Place the chicken breast on the bottom of your crock pot.
3. In a large bowl mix together cream of chicken soup, onion soup mix, frozen vegetables, potatoes, chicken broth and tarragon. Pour over the chicken.
4. Top with butter. Cover with lid and cook 3 hours on high or 6 hours on low.
5. Temporarily remove the chicken breasts to a plate and with 2 forks pull the chicken apart in small pieces. Add chicken back to crock pot and mix in.
6. Tear the refrigerator raw biscuit dough into pieces and place it on top of the chicken mixture in the crock pot.
7. Cover with lid and cook an additional 1½ hours on high.

Caramel Apple Pecan French Toast

Serves 8

Ingredients:
1 loaf French bread
6 eggs
1 ½ cups milk
1 ½ teaspoon cinnamon
½ cup butter
1 cup brown sugar
2 tablespoons corn syrup
1 teaspoon vanilla extract
½ teaspoon almond extract

Topping:
¼ cup pecan halves
1 granny smith apple, peeled, cored, and diced
¼ teaspoon salt

Maple Syrup (optional)

There are many ways to make your breakfast special, and this apple pecan French toast will have your family asking for more!

1. Take loaf of French bread, cut it into cubes and place the bread cubes into a large bowl.
2. In a different bowl, place your eggs, milk, and cinnamon and beat together until well blended.
3. Pour your egg and milk mixture over your bread cubes and mix until all your bread is well coated.
4. Cover and place in your refrigerator for at least 4 hours or overnight.
5. Mix together your butter, brown sugar, corn syrup, vanilla and almond extract. Cover and place in your refrigerator until needed.
6. Grease your crock pot.
7. Pour your coated bread into your greased crock pot.
8. Pour and spread butter mixture over the bread.
9. Add topping to crock pot.
10. Cover with lid and cook 2 hours on high or 4 hours on low. Let it cool down for about 15-20 minutes before serving. Drizzle with maple syrup (optional)

GERMAN

German Chocolate Brownies page 55

The cuisine of Germany has evolved as a national cuisine through centuries of social and political change with variations from region to region. Some regions of Germany, like Bavaria and neighboring Swabia, share dishes with Austrian and parts of Swiss cuisine.

The Michelin Guide of 2015 awarded eleven restaurants in Germany three stars, the highest designation, while 38 more received two stars and 233 one star. According to the Guide, one star signifies "a very good restaurant", two stars are "excellent cooking that is worth a detour", and three stars mean "exceptional cuisine that is worth a special journey". The listing of starred restaurants is updated once a year. German restaurants have become the world's second-most decorated after France.

Split Pea Soup

Serves 6

Ingredients:
1 large onion, chopped
2 teaspoons minced garlic
2 tablespoons olive oil
½ teaspoon dried oregano
1 ½ teaspoons kosher salt
1 teaspoon ground black pepper
3 carrots, peeled and diced
3 celery stalks, diced
1 pound bag dried split green peas
1 meaty smoked ham bone or 2 ham hocks and any leftover ham shoulder meat.
8 cups chicken stock

Pea soup is a common dish throughout Germany. It often contains meat such as bacon, sausage or Kassler (cured smoked pork) depending on regional preferences. Very often, several Würste (sausage) will accompany a serving of pea soup as well as some dark bread. Something magical happens when dried split peas break down into a thick, naturally creamy, and delicious soup over several hours in the slow cooker. Add everything to your crock pot, and you're on your way to making the ultimate comforting soup. One day I cooked a very large ham for dinner. All the left-over ham made for a delicious soup. This soup freezes well, so make a batch and save extra for later.

1. Mix all ingredients in crock pot.
2. Cover with lid and cook 5 hours on high or 10 hours on low.

Schweinebraten (Bavarian Pork Roast)

Serves 6

Ingredients:
4-5 lbs boneless pork roast
2 tablespoons olive oil
¼ cup Dijon mustard
¼ cup dry white wine
1 bottle of dark Weissber beer or other dark beer
1 cup vegetable broth
1 tablespoon minced garlic
2 medium onions, quartered
3 medium potatoes, peeled and quartered
1 small red cabbage, core removed, cut into quarters
2 tablespoons cornstarch

Pork Dry Rub: Mix together
¼ teaspoon caraway seed, ground
¼ teaspoon onion powder
¼ teaspoon garlic powder
½ teaspoon paprika
¼ teaspoon celery salt
1 teaspoon salt
½ teaspoon ground black pepper

This is the delicious Bavarian Pork Roast. Juicy and very tender with a fantastic sauce. Traditionally served with potato dumplings and sauerkraut.

1. Rub dry rub onto roast.
2. Spread mustard onto roast.
3. Heat olive oil in a pan on medium high heat and brown roast on all sides.
4. When roast is browned, add wine and beer to deglaze pan.
5. Add the roast with the juices from the pan to your crock pot.
6. Add the vegetable broth, garlic, onions, potatoes, and cabbage.
7. Cover with lid and cook 4 hours on high or 8 hours on low.
8. Remove the cooked pork roast and vegetables.

In a cup, add cornstarch with 3 tablespoons of liquid form the crock pot, stir until smooth and then mix into the crock pot to thicken the gravy.

Sauerbraten (Beef Pot Roast)

Serves 2

Ingredients:
1 pound beef stew meat
1 small onion, chopped
2 carrots, sliced
½ cup diced celery
2 tablespoons brown sugar
(firmly packed)
9 old-fashioned gingersnaps
(about 2.5 ounces), crushed

Marinade:
1 cups water
½ cup cider vinegar
1 cup beef broth
2 teaspoons salt
¼ teaspoon ground black pepper
1 bay leaves
¼ teaspoon dry ground clove
¼ teaspoon dry ground mustard
2 tablespoons Gin

A German pot roast that can be prepared with a variety of meats, most often beef, but also venison, lamb, and pork. The ingredients of the marinade vary based on regional styles and traditions throughout Germany. Sauerbraten is regarded as one of the best-known German meals because of German immigration to the United States. It is frequently found on the menus of German-style restaurants in America.

1. Mix together the marinade and marinate the beef in this mixture in your refrigerator overnight.
2. Heat 1 tablespoon of oil in a pan over medium high heat and brown the meat. Reserve the marinade.
3. Add beef with marinade to your crock pot.
4. Mix in onions, carrots, and celery in crock pot.
5. Cover with lid and cook 3 hours on high or 6 hours on low.
6. Discard bay leaves and mix in the brown sugar and crushed gingersnap.
7. Cook an additional hour on high.

Jagerschnitzel (Pork Cutlets)

Serves 4

Ingredients:
4 boneless pork cutlets, ¼ inch thick
1 cup all-purpose flour
1 tablespoon salt
½ teaspoon ground black pepper
1 teaspoon granulated garlic
1 teaspoon paprika
1 egg
½ cup milk
2 teaspoons mustard
1 cup crushed unsalted Saltine crackers
1 cup panko bread crumbs
½ pound bacon, diced
½ cup olive oil, for frying
½ diced yellow onion,
2 cups sliced mushrooms
¼ cup red wine
2 cups beef stock
4 tablespoons butter, room temperature

This is a famous German dish that tourists go home raving about. This dish was originally made with venison or wild boar. It's now normally made with pork. It takes a little work to prepare, but it's so good, you'll find yourself making it again. The melted butter on top finishes it off!

1. In a medium bowl, mix together the flour, salt, pepper, garlic and paprika.
2. In another bowl, beat egg, milk, and mustard together.
3. In another bowl, combine cracker and panko crumbs.
4. Dredge pork cutlets first in flour, then in egg wash, and finally in cracker panko crumbs.
5. In a medium sauté pan over medium heat cook the bacon until crispy. Remove bacon from pan to drain on paper towels.
6. In same pan with bacon fat and olive oil. Heat oil over medium-high in large sauté pan or cast iron skillet. Cook pork evenly on both sides till brown. As each piece of pork is done, add to your crock pot.
7. Add onion, mushrooms, wine, and beef stock to your crock pot over the pork.
8. Cover with lid and cook 3 hours on high or 6 hours on low.

To serve, cover pork cutlets with mushroom gravy from crock pot. Sprinkle with cooked chopped bacon and 1 tablespoon of butter for each dish.

Gruenkohl und Pinkel (Kale and Sausage)

Serves 4

Ingredients:
¾ - 1 pound kale leaves fresh or
frozen, chopped
2 onions, chopped
½ pound thick bacon, sliced into
1 inch pieces
8 links of sausage, total (Choose
from - Bratwurst, Knackwurst,
Bregenwurst, Bockwurst)
2 large potatoes, peeled and
quartered
1 teaspoon ground mustard
1 tablespoon butter
½ teaspoon salt
¼ teaspoon ground black pepper
⅛ teaspoon allspice
2 ½ cups vegetable broth
2 tablespoons oatmeal

Pinkel is a smoked Kaszanka, a type of sausage which is eaten with kale. It is eaten mainly in northwest Germany. Cooked kale is mixed with mustard, bacon, sausage and potatoes for a delicious dinner.

1. Mix all ingredients in crock pot EXCEPT Oatmeal.
2. Cover with lid and cook 3 hours on high or 6 hours on low.
3. Mix in oatmeal to crock pot and cook on high an additional 30 minutes.

Chocolate Brownies

Serves 14 brownies

Ingredients:
½ cup butter
4 oz. German sweet chocolate,
coarsely chopped
2 large eggs, lightly beaten
1 teaspoon vanilla extract
1 cup all-purpose flour
½ cup sugar
½ teaspoon baking powder
¼ teaspoon salt

Topping:
2 tablespoons butter, melted
½ cup packed brown sugar
1 cup flaked coconut
½ cup chopped pecans
2 tablespoons corn syrup
2 tablespoons milk

These German Chocolate Brownies are the BEST! Rich chocolaty brownies topped with a gooey homemade coconut pecan topping.

1. In a microwave, melt butter and chocolate; in 30-second increments, stirring after each, until chocolate is melted. cool slightly, stir in beaten eggs and vanilla extract.
2. Lightly coat a 5-quart slow-cooker with cooking spray.
3. Line bottom with parchment paper and lightly coat with spray.
4. In a small bowl, whisk together flour, sugar, baking powder, and salt.
5. Add flour mixture to the chocolate egg mixture and stir just until moistened (do not overmix).
6. Transfer to slow cooker and smooth top.
7. Cover and cook on low, 3 ½ hours.
8. For topping, combine butter and brown sugar in a large bowl. Add coconut, pecans, corn syrup and milk; mix well. When the 3 ½ hour cooking time is up in your crock pot, drop topping by teaspoonful onto warm brownies; spread evenly.
9. Leave crock pot uncover and cook an additional 30 minutes.
10. Remove insert from slow cooker and run a knife around edge to loosen brownies. Let cool completely about 2 hours. Turn out onto a work surface and cut into 14 brownies.

Apple Butter

Serves 4 pint jars

Ingredients:
**5 ½ pounds granny smith apples -
peeled, cored and finely chopped**
4 cups white sugar
2 teaspoons ground cinnamon
¼ teaspoon ground cloves
¼ teaspoon salt

Apple butter has been a method for preserving fruit since ancient Greece. Cooking or rendering fruit until the sugar content is above 50%, preserves it, often without canning or refrigeration. The Germans and Dutch make and eat a similar product from pressed fruit, called Apfelkraut. In Rhineland, where traditional apple orchards grow, it is considered a specialty.

1. Place the apples in a crock pot.
2. In a medium bowl, mix the sugar, cinnamon, cloves, and salt.
3. Pour the mixture over the apples in the crock pot and mix well.
4. Cover with lid and cook 1 hour on high.
5. Reduce heat to low and cook 10 hours, stirring occasionally, until the mixture is thickened and dark brown.
6. Uncover and continue cooking on low 1 hour. Stir with a whisk, to increase smoothness.

Spoon the mixture into sterile containers, cover and refrigerate or freeze.

INDIAN

Chicken Tikka Masala page 62

Indian cuisine encompasses a wide variety of regional and traditional cuisines native to India. India has a range of diversity in soil, climate, culture, and occupations. The cuisines vary from each other because of locally available spices, herbs, vegetables, and fruits.

Religious and cultural choices and traditions influence Indian food. There has been Middle Eastern and Central Asian influence on North Indian cuisine. Indian cuisine is still evolving because of the nation's cultural interactions with other societies.

Historical incidents such as foreign invasions, trade relations and colonialism have played a role in introducing foods to the country. For instance, the potato, a staple of the diet in some regions of India, was brought to India by the Portuguese, who introduced chilies and breadfruit.

Indian cuisine has shaped the history of international relations. The spice trade between India and Europe was the primary catalyst for Europe's Age of Discovery. Spices are bought from India and traded around Europe and Asia. Indian cuisine has influenced other cuisines across the world, especially those from Middle East, North Africa, Southeast Asia, the British Isles, Fiji, and the Caribbean.

Chicken Vindaloo

Serves 4

Ingredients:
2 pounds boneless chicken cut into chunks
1 teaspoon salt
½ teaspoons ground black pepper
1 tablespoon olive oil
1 tablespoon minced garlic
3 onions, chopped
1 teaspoon powdered ginger
2 teaspoons cumin powder
2 teaspoon dry ground mustard
1 teaspoon ground cinnamon
½ teaspoon ground cloves
1 teaspoon turmeric
½ teaspoon cayenne pepper
1 tablespoon paprika
2 teaspoons lemon juice
2 tablespoons distilled white vinegar
1 tablespoon brown sugar
1 cup tomato sauce
1 cup water
Garnish - chopped cilantro

This is a tangy, hot, spicy curry dish from Goa, India. This recipe is easy and delicious! While packed with flavor, Vindaloo is one of the hottest dishes you can order at an Indian food restaurant. If you don't like heat, then you will not like this dish. If you do, then you may have found heaven. If you like things Hot and Spicy there won't be any leftovers.

1. Add and mix everything together in crock pot.
2. Cover with lid and cook 4 hours on high or 8 hours on low.

Garnish with cilantro.
Serve with steamed cauliflower or white rice.

Cranberry Chicken Curry

Serves 4

Ingredients:
2 pounds boneless, skinless chicken breasts
2 teaspoons curry powder
1 tablespoon butter
2 onions, chopped
1 tablespoon minced garlic
1 teaspoon dry ground mustard
¼ teaspoon ground clove
1 ⅓ cups sweetened dried cranberries
1 teaspoon dry ground ginger
1 teaspoon salt
½ teaspoon ground black pepper
¼ teaspoon cayenne pepper
1 (14.5 ounce can) diced tomatoes
1 (4.5 ounce can) chopped green chilies
1 ½ cups chicken broth
Garnish - chopped cilantro

This is one of those amazing recipes made with cranberries, green chilies, ginger, and garlic. Cranberry curry dish that combines for a sweet, savory take on chicken curry. The dried cranberries, tomatoes, mustard, and fragrant curry spices brighten this zesty Indian dish. The mouthwatering flavors of the exotic sauce will bring you back for a second helping.

Directions:
1. Add and mix everything together in crock pot.
2. Cover with lid and cook 4 hours on high or 8 hours on low.

Garnish with cilantro.

Chicken Tikka Makhani

Serves 4

Ingredients:
2 pounds boneless chicken cut into bite size pieces
1 small onion, chopped
3 tablespoons butter
2 teaspoons lemon juice
1 tablespoon minced garlic
1 teaspoon chili powder
¼ teaspoon cayenne pepper
1 bay leaf
1 ½ teaspoons salt
½ teaspoon ground black pepper
1 teaspoon ground cumin
½ teaspoon ground ginger
½ teaspoons ground coriander
¼ teaspoon ground cinnamon
¼ teaspoon ground cloves
¼ teaspoon ground nutmeg
1 cup tomato puree
¼ cup water
¼ cup plain yogurt
3 tablespoons heavy cream
Garnish with chopped cilantro

This butter chicken dish has a mildly spiced curry sauce. It tastes incredible! The dish has its roots in Punjabi cuisine and was developed by a restaurant in Delhi. It is a full-flavored dish that complements the chicken well. You can make this as mild or spicy as you wish by adjusting the cayenne. It's so good that you may have to stop ordering it at Indian Restaurants and make it yourself! Serve with cooked basmati rice.

1. Add and mix everything together in crock pot EXCEPT yogurt and heavy cream.
2. Cover with lid and cook 4 hours on high or 8 hours on low.
3. Mix in yogurt and heavy cream and serve.

Garnish with cilantro.

Chicken Dum Aloo

Serves 4

Ingredients:
2 pounds boneless chicken cut into bite size pieces
12 baby potatoes
1 large onion, sliced
¼ teaspoon dry ground ginger
1 tablespoon minced garlic
2 tablespoons raisins
4 green chilies, sliced
½ teaspoon ground cinnamon
¼ teaspoon dry ground clove
1 bay leaf
½ teaspoon chili powder
¼ teaspoon turmeric powder
¼ teaspoon garlic powder
1 cup water
1 teaspoon salt
½ teaspoon ground black pepper
½ cup yogurt

Dum Aloo (also spelled as Dam Aloo) or Alu Dum is a dish from India. Dum Aloo is a creamy curry, usually made with baby potatoes, were the potatoes are slow cooked in a spicy sauce. This cooking method is referred to as 'dum'. The slow cooking process lets the potatoes absorb all the flavor from the curry. Dum Aloo is a popular recipe cooked throughout India.

Directions:
1. Add and mix everything together in crock pot EXCEPT yogurt.
2. Cover with lid and cook 4 hours on high or 8 hours on low.
3. Mix in yogurt and serve.

Chicken Tikka Masala

Serves 4

Ingredients:
2 pounds boneless chicken cut into bite size pieces
1 large onion, diced
1 green bell pepper, deveined, seeded cut into chunks
1 teaspoon lemon juice
1 tablespoon crushed garlic
1 tablespoon butter
½ teaspoon turmeric powder
¼ teaspoon coriander powder
¼ teaspoon ground cumin powder
¼ teaspoon ground ginger powder
¼ teaspoon ground nutmeg powder
1 ½ teaspoons salt
½ teaspoon ground black pepper
¼ teaspoon cayenne pepper
¼ teaspoon cinnamon
1 tablespoons brown sugar
1 cup of water mixed with 2 tablespoons tomato paste
2 ½ tablespoons plain, Greek yogurt
3 tablespoons heavy cream
Garnish with chopped cilantro

If there's one dish guaranteed to be on every Indian restaurant menu, its chicken tikka masala. It has chunks of chicken enveloped in a creamy spiced tomato sauce. This dish has tremendous popularity. When the dish is eaten with naan bread, it's like an Indian version of pizza! Preparing it at home, you get the added bonus of a kitchen infused with intoxicating aromas.

Directions:
1. Add and mix everything together in crock pot EXCEPT yogurt and cream.
2. Cover with lid and cook 4 hours on high or 8 hours on low.
3. Mix in yogurt and cream and serve.

IRISH

Corned Beef and Cabbage page 66

Irish cuisine is a style of cooking originating from Ireland or developed by Irish people. It evolved from centuries of social and political change. The cuisine takes its influence from the crops grown and animals farmed in its temperate climate.

The introduction of the potato in the second half of the 16th century heavily influenced Ireland's cuisine thereafter and, as a result, is often closely associated with Ireland. Representative Irish dishes include Irish stew, bacon, and cabbage, coddle, and colcannon. You're going to want to eat these recipes way beyond St. Patrick's Day.

Modern Irish dishes include Irish stew (made with lamb, mutton, or goat), shepherd's pie (meat and vegetables, topped with potato), bacon and cabbage (with potatoes), and coddle (sausage, bacon, and potato).

Red Potatoes

Serves 8

Ingredients:
2 pounds red potatoes, cut into wedges
½ cup water
½ cup butter
1 tablespoon lemon juice
1 teaspoon dried parsley
2 green onions, sliced
2 teaspoons dried dill
1 teaspoon salt
¼ teaspoon ground black pepper

This Slow Cooker Irish Potatoes Recipe is one of those slow cooker potato recipes that's easy to make, and is sure to impress your guests. It even would be a great potluck dish! These potatoes bring a touch of Ireland to your kitchen and they go with almost every main dish. This is a terrific slow cooker side dish recipe to prepare at the last minute. Very simple to make and everyone loves the flavor.

1. Add all the ingredients to your crock pot.
2. Cover with lid and cook 3 hours on high or 6 hours on low.

Coddle (Sausage Stew)

Serves 4

Ingredients:
1 pound pork sausage links, sliced
½ pound smoked bacon, cubed
2 onions, thinly sliced
3 carrots, peeled and chopped
2 large potatoes, peeled cut into wedges
1 teaspoon salt
½ teaspoon ground black pepper
1 cup beef stock
1 bottle Irish stout beer (such as Guinness)

This traditional supper dish of sausages, bacon, onions, and potatoes dates back at least as far as the early eighteenth century. This traditional recipe brings you Irish comfort food in a sauce made with Irish stout.

1. Add all the ingredients to your crock pot.
2. Cover with lid and cook 4 hours on high or 8 hours on low.

Corned Beef and Cabbage

Serves 4

Ingredients:
3-4 pound Corned-Beef Brisket
4 cups water
2 bottles Irish stout beer (such as Guinness)
4 carrots, sliced
2 onions sliced in half
2 large potatoes, quartered
1 small head cabbage, cut in wedges
1 Spice packet (if your corned beef did not come with a spice packet, use 2 teaspoons of pickling spice)

Corned beef and cabbage is the tradition on St. Patrick's Day, an event that is more common in America. Surprisingly, corned beef and cabbage is not a tradition in Ireland. It is an Irish-American-Jewish tradition. Irish immigrants in the US found beef more plentiful than lamb.

It's a shame the dish is not served more often. Corned beef and cabbage makes a delicious dinner any time or day of the year.

1. Add all the ingredients to your crock pot.
2. Cover with lid and cook 4 hours on high or 8 hours on low.

Shepherd's Pie

Serves 4

Ingredients:
3 pounds ground beef
5 russet potatoes peeled, cut into quarters
1 teaspoon salt
½ teaspoon ground black pepper
1 tablespoon milk
2 tablespoon butter
1 onion chopped
2 - (.87 oz.) dry brown gravy mix packages
1 cup water
½ teaspoon garlic powder
½ teaspoon onion powder
1 (10.5 oz.) can cream of mushroom soup
2 cups frozen whole kernel corn, not thawed
½ teaspoon paprika
2 tablespoons cold butter

In the United States, the dish can vary widely, whether as a home recipe or a standard menu item in an Irish pub. If you add ground lamb the Irish call it Cottage Pie. Your family will love this easy recipe. This recipe offers all the comfort of a classic shepherd pie recipe, yet can simmer all day while you are working away or cook and carry to you next family gathering. Rich savory shepherd's pie will keep guests coming back for seconds.

1. Boil your potatoes, drain and mash with salt, pepper, milk, and butter, set aside. Mashed potatoes may seem dry, but they will become moist while in the crock pot.
2. In a large skillet, cook beef over medium heat, 10 minutes, breaking up beef into crumbles, then drain.
3. Spray your crock pot with cooking spray.
4. Add cooked beef to your crock pot and mix together with onion, brown gravy mixes, water, garlic powder, onion powder, and cream of mushroom soup. Mix thoroughly.
5. Add frozen corn over beef mixture.
6. Spoon your mashed potatoes on top and spread evenly.
7. Sprinkle paprika over potatoes.
8. Top with butter, sliced and scattered around top of potatoes.
9. Cover with lid and cook 4 hours on high or 8 hours on low.

Guinness Pie

Serves 4

Ingredients:
1 pound beef stew meat
2 slices bacon, chopped
1 onion, chopped
1 carrot, sliced
1 (8 oz.) package sliced
mushrooms
1 teaspoon minced garlic
1 teaspoon sugar
1 ½ tablespoons all-purpose flour
1 bottle Irish stout beer (such as
Guinness)
1 cup beef stock
¼ teaspoon ground thyme
2 bay leaves

Topping:
1 (16.3 oz.) flaky buttermilk
biscuits, like Pillsbury

This recipe comes from Ireland. It's a delicious traditional beef and mushroom dish and a great way to get the Irish stout into your stew. It gives the dish a very rich flavor. A one-pot meal that the entire family will enjoy.

1. Mix in all the ingredients to your crock pot.
2. Cover with lid and cook 4 hours on high or 8 hours on low.
3. Bake biscuits per package directions.

Remove bay leaves.
Serve - Slice one or two biscuits in half and serve with the stew in the middle.

Cabbage, Potatoes and Bacon

Serves 4

Ingredients:
4 cups cabbage, chopped
1 small onion, chopped
2 medium potatoes, peeled and chopped
1 teaspoon caraway seeds
1 teaspoon salt
½ teaspoon ground black pepper
4 strips thick bacon, chopped
1 bottle Irish lager beer (such as Guinness)
1 cup chicken stock

Garnish with parsley

Still popular in Ireland today is this traditional dish of cabbage and potatoes. This is the original, much-loved dish that Irish immigrants of the nineteenth century missed when they came to North America. The addition of bacon just put this version over the top.

1. Spray crock pot with nonstick cooking spray.
2. Place cabbage in bottom of slow cooker; add onion and toss gently.
3. Add potatoes, caraway seeds, salt, and pepper.
4. Add bacon over potatoes and pour the beer and chicken stock on top.
5. Cover with lid and cook 4 hours on high or 8 hours on low.

Garnish with parsley.

Apple Crumble

Serves 6

Ingredients:
For the Apples:
6 Granny Smith Apples peeled, cored, and sliced
Juice of 1 lemon
1 teaspoon cinnamon
¼ cup white sugar
½ teaspoon baking powder
1 teaspoon vanilla extract

Topping:
½ cup dry oats (instant or rolled)
½ cup all-purpose flour
¾ cup brown sugar
¼ cup white sugar
1 teaspoon cinnamon
¼ teaspoon salt
8 tablespoon butter, cut into small pieces

With a chill in the air and the trees awash with autumn colors. It's the perfect dessert to tuck into something warm and tasty during the cold months. Super easy to make and guaranteed to be a treat. The traditional Irish apple crumble is the ideal Winter warmer dish, but I think it's a delicious dessert any time of year.

1. Place sliced apples in your crock pot.
2. Add lemon juice, cinnamon, white sugar, baking powder, and vanilla extract. Stir until apples are evenly coated.
3. Topping - in a mixing bowl, add oats, flour, brown sugar, white sugar, cinnamon, and salt. Stir to combine all ingredients.
4. Add butter into flour mixture. Using a spoon or your hands, combine flour mixture and butter until it forms a dough.
5. Crumble dough on top of apples evenly.
6. Cover with lid and cook 2 hours on high or 4 hours on low.
7. Open lid part way and cook for an additional hour to let top get "crispy".

Serve warm and top with vanilla ice cream if desired.

ITALIAN

Lasagna page 81

Italian cuisine has developed through centuries of social and political changes, with roots stretching to antiquity. Significant changes occurred with the discovery of the New World and the introduction of potatoes, tomatoes, bell peppers and maize. Italian cuisine is noted for its regional diversity, abundance of difference in taste, and is one of the most popular in the world, with influences abroad.

Italian cuisine is characterized by its simplicity, with many dishes having only four to eight ingredients. Italian cooks rely chiefly on the quality of the ingredients rather than on elaborate preparation. Ingredients and dishes vary by region. Many dishes that were once regional, however, have proliferated with variations throughout the country.

Cheese and wine are a major part of the cuisine, with many variations. Coffee, specifically espresso, has become important in Italian cuisine.

Zuppa Toscana (Sausage Soup)

Serves 6

Ingredients:
1 pound ground Italian sausage, or links, casings removed and crumbled
3 russet potatoes, peeled, cut into bite size pieces.
2 teaspoons minced garlic
1 large white onion, finely chopped
4 cups chicken broth
½ teaspoon salt
¼ teaspoon ground black pepper
1 cup kale leaves, chopped
1 cup heavy cream

Garnish:
4 strips of bacon, cooked and chopped

You don't have to venture to your favorite Italian restaurant to get this classic, slow-cooked sausage and potato soup. Heavy whipping cream is the key to rich, full-bodied flavor. Use Spicy Italian Sausage to get that signature Italian restaurant flavor.

1. Cook bacon till crisp and set aside for later.
2. Brown Italian sausage in a large skillet over medium-high heat, about 5 minutes. Drain and discard fat.
3. Combine cooked sausage and all other ingredients EXCEPT cream, bacon, and kale in your crock pot.
4. Cover with lid and cook 3 hours on high or 6 hours on low.
5. Add cream and kale to crock pot, stir, and cook an additional hour on high.

Garnish with cooked chopped bacon.

Tomato Sausage Soup

Serves 6

Ingredients:
2 slices bacon, diced
1 pound ground Italian sausage, or links, casings removed and crumbled
2 medium sized carrots, chopped
1 cup chopped red onion
1 teaspoon salt
½ teaspoon black pepper
¼ teaspoon crushed red pepper flakes
1 tablespoons minced garlic
1 bay leaf
4 cups crushed tomatoes
3 cups chicken stock
¼ cup finely chopped fresh parsley leaves

A wonderful soup! Very quick and very easy and so tasty! This soup is hearty and satisfying.

1. Add all ingredients to crock pot EXCEPT parsley and mix together.
2. Cover with lid and cook 4 hours on high or 8 hours on low.
3. Stir in parsley and serve.

Pasta e Fagioli (Pasta and Beans)

Serves 4

Ingredients:
½ pound ground beef
1 small onion, diced
1 carrot, peeled and sliced
2 stalks celery, chopped
2 teaspoons minced garlic
1 (14.5-ounce) cans diced tomatoes
1 can red kidney beans (with liquid)
1 can great northern beans (with liquid)
3 cups beef broth
1 (8 oz.) can tomato sauce
1 can (5.5 oz.) V-8 juice
½ tablespoon white vinegar
½ teaspoon salt
¼ teaspoon dried oregano
½ teaspoon dried basil
¼ teaspoon ground black pepper
¼ pound of Ditalini pasta
A pinch of dried thyme

Pasta e fagioli, meaning "pasta and beans", is a traditional meatless Italian dish. Like many other Italian favorites including pizza and polenta, the dish started as a peasant dish, being composed of inexpensive ingredients. Today it can be widely found, even in restaurants that do not specialize in Italian cuisine. This recipe can easily be doubled to serve more guests.

1. In a large skillet, cook beef over medium heat, 10 minutes, breaking up beef into crumbles, then drain.
2. Add the beef and all the other ingredients to your crock pot, EXCEPT pasta.
3. Cover with lid and cook 3 hours on high or 6 hours on low.
4. Mix in pasta and cook an additional hour on high.

Spicy Meatball and Sausage

Serves 4

Ingredients:
1 ½ lbs. ground beef
1 large onion chopped
1 ½ teaspoons salt
½ teaspoon black pepper
2 teaspoons of crushed garlic
¼ teaspoon crushed hot red pepper
¼ teaspoon dry ground basil
¼ teaspoon dry ground oregano
2 large eggs

1 cup grated parmesan cheese
2-5 links of Italian sausage
1 jar of your favorite pasta sauce
½ cup of water

These meatballs have no breadcrumb, which gives them a real meat texture and its low carb too! Meatball recipes are often challenged by chefs who claim, "Mine are the best!" Try them for yourself! Cooked with your favorite sausage makes this a hearty delicious meal.

1. In a bowl mix together the first 9 ingredients.
2. Then add grated Parmesan cheese and mix well.
3. Roll into meatballs and add the meatballs to an oven safe dish. Cook meatballs in the oven at 375F until well browned on both sides.
4. Add cooked meatballs, uncooked sausage, pasta sauce, and water to your crock pot.
5. Cover with lid and cook 4 hours on high or 8 hours on low.

Garnish with some grated parmesan and parsley.

Stuffed Peppers

Serves 4

Ingredients:
4 medium bell peppers (any color)
½ pound ground Italian sausage, uncooked
1 small onion, chopped
½ cup instant white rice, uncooked
2 tablespoons grated parmesan cheese
2 teaspoons minced garlic
¼ teaspoon dried oregano
1 jar of your favorite pasta sauce, divided
½ teaspoon salt
¼ teaspoon ground black pepper
1 package shredded Italian five cheeses, divided
¼ cup water

This truly is the best stuffed peppers recipe! Filled with Italian sausage and rice. These stuffed peppers are savory and delicious.

1. Cut tops off peppers; remove and discard seeds.
2. Chop tops, add to medium bowl, add sausage, onion, rice, parmesan cheese, garlic, oregano, 1 ½ cups sauce, salt, pepper and 1 ¼ cups shredded cheese; mix lightly.
3. Spoon stuffing into pepper shells.
4. Pour water into the bottom of your crock pot.
5. Stand peppers in slow cooker; top with remaining sauce and shredded cheese.
6. Cover with lid and cook 3 hours on high or 6 hours on low.

Sausage, Peppers and Onions

Serves 6

Ingredients:
2 packages of sweet Italian sausage, sliced (2 pounds total) uncooked
3 onions, sliced
1 green bell pepper, sliced
1 red bell pepper, sliced
1 yellow bell pepper, sliced
1 orange bell pepper, sliced
1 ½ teaspoons salt
½ teaspoon ground black pepper
¼ teaspoon dried oregano
½ teaspoons ground dry basil
1 tablespoon minced garlic
1 cup tomato sauce
½ cup red wine
¼ teaspoon hot red pepper flakes

This is one of those classic Italian cater-food dishes. It's so good. Italian sausages cooked with bell peppers, onions, crushed tomatoes, and garlic. Served in a hoagie roll, over pasta or just as it is.

1. Mix all ingredients in crock pot.
2. Cover with lid and cook 4 hours on high or 8 hours on low.

Balsamic Chicken

Serves 4

Ingredients:
8 boneless chicken thighs, skin removed
1 jar of your favorite pasta sauce
1 tablespoon olive oil
1 tablespoon minced garlic
1 teaspoon salt
½ teaspoon ground black pepper
½ teaspoon garlic powder
1 teaspoon dried basil
½ cup balsamic vinegar
1 tablespoon honey
1 onion, sliced

Looking for an easy dinner to whip up that's healthy and delicious. Try this easy one pat balsamic chicken that comes together quickly and tastes delicious. Balsamic vinegar, with its hallmark dark color, syrupy body, and slight sweetness, brings a wonderful out-of-the-ordinary touch to any recipe.

1. Mix all ingredients in crock pot.
2. Cover with lid and cook 4 hours on high or 8 hours on low.

American Chop Suey

Serves 6

Ingredients:
1 tablespoons olive oil
1 pound ground beef
2 medium onions, chopped
1 green pepper, chopped
½ pound ground Italian sausage, or links, casings removed and crumbled
½ cup ketchup
1 jar of your favorite pasta sauce
1 ½ teaspoon salt
½ teaspoon black pepper
3 cups water
½ cup red wine
½ pound elbow macaroni (which is a half box of the 1 pound box of store bought pasta)

This is a classic American pasta dish. Chop suey consists of elbow macaroni, cooked ground beef, onions, and green peppers in a tomato-based sauce. Though Italian-American cuisine clearly influences this American comfort food, it is known as "American chop suey" because it's sometimes a hodgepodge of leftover meat and vegetables. This recipe is quite adaptable to taste and available ingredients. Elbow macaroni is the standard but can be substituted with pasta of similar size, such as ziti, farfalle, or rotelle. This recipe includes sausage that adds to the flavor.

1. Heat oil in a pan and cook the ground beef till no longer pink and drain the oil, then add beef to crock pot.
2. Add and mix all other ingredients together in crock pot, EXCEPT elbow macaroni.
3. Cover with lid and cook 3 hours on high or 6 hours on low.
4. Mix in uncooked elbow macaroni and cook an additional hour.

Chicken Cacciatore

Serves 4

Ingredients:
6 skinless chicken thighs, bone-in
1 teaspoon salt
½ teaspoon ground black pepper
1 tablespoon minced garlic
1 onion, sliced
1 orange bell pepper, sliced
1 red bell pepper, sliced
1 (8 oz.) package mushrooms, sliced
¼ teaspoon dry thyme leaves
1 teaspoon dried parsley
1 teaspoon dried basil
¼ teaspoon dried oregano
½ cup red wine
1 (28 oz.) can crushed tomatoes
2 tablespoons tomato paste
½ teaspoon red pepper flakes

In cuisine, alla cacciatora refers to a meal prepared "hunter-style" with onions, herbs, usually tomatoes, often bell peppers, and sometimes wine. Cacciatore was named for the Italian poet Antonio Cacciatore. Slow cooked chicken cacciatore, with chicken falling off the bone in a rich and rustic sauce is simple Italian comfort food at its best. Chicken Cacciatore is a classic, but you'll never get a more succulent home cooked meal than this recipe!

1. Mix all ingredients in crock pot.
2. Cover with lid and cook 4 hours on high or 8 hours on low.

Serve over Polenta if desired.

Lasagna

Serves 4

Ingredients:
1 pound ground beef
1 jar of your favorite pasta sauce.
1 cup water
1 container (15 oz.) ricotta cheese
1 package (7 oz.) shredded
mozzarella cheese, divided
¼ cup grated parmesan cheese,
divided
1 egg
2 tablespoons chopped fresh
parsley
6 lasagna noodles, uncooked,
divided

Lasagna is a homemade comfort food tradition that the whole family loves, and this slow-cooker version is a must-try. I'm sure everyone has their own favorite lasagna recipe, but this really is the best lasagna ever. Anyone can make this, anywhere, anytime. And it's the easiest thing in the world. You don't even have to cook the noodles first.

1. Brown meat in large skillet; drain. Stir in pasta sauce and water.
2. Mix ricotta, 1 ½ cups mozzarella, 2 tablespoons of the. Parmesan, egg, and parsley.
3. Spoon 1 cup meat sauce into slow cooker; followed by a layer of 3 noodles (break noodles to fit).
4. Spread ½ the cheese mixture over noodles.
5. Cover with 2 cups meat sauce.
6. Top with remaining noodles (break noodles to fit).
7. Add rest of cheese mixture and meat sauce.
8. Cover with lid and cook on low 4 to 6 hours or until noodles absorb the liquid.
9. Sprinkle with both remaining cheeses; let stand, covered, for about ten minutes or until melted.

Tiramisu Bread Pudding

Serves 6

Ingredients:
½ cup water
½ cup granulated sugar
1 tablespoon instant espresso
2 tablespoons Kahlua
1 ½ cups whole milk
½ cup heavy cream
5 large eggs
8 cups cubed (1-inch pieces)
French bread

Topping:
½ cup heavy cream
⅓ cup mascarpone cheese
1 tablespoon granulated sugar
1 teaspoon vanilla extract

Garnish:
Unsweetened cocoa, for dusting

This must be one of the most fabulous dessert recipes! If you love bread pudding, tiramisu and mascarpone cheese this will be one of your favorite desserts ever!

1. Generously spray your crockpot with nonstick cooking spray.
2. In a small saucepan, add the water, sugar, and espresso. Bring the mixture to a boil over medium high heat, stirring until the sugar dissolves. Once boiling, remove from the heat. Stir in the Kahlua. Set aside and let cool for about 15 minutes.
3. In a large bowl, add the milk, cream, and eggs. Whisk until well combined. Add in the cooled espresso mixture, whisking to combine.
4. Add in the bread cubes and mix until all the bread is coated with the mixture.
5. Transfer the mixture to your crockpot.
6. Cover and cook on low for about 2 hours or until set.

Topping – Add all these ingredients to a bowl. Beat on high until thickened (and some peaks form – it won't be as stiff as whipped cream).

To serve – scoop the bread pudding into bowls. Add a generous amount of the topping and then dust with the cocoa powder.

JAPANESE

Supearibu no Nikomi (Braised Spare Ribs) page 84

Japanese cuisine has developed through centuries of social and economic changes. It encompasses the regional and traditional foods of Japan. The traditional cuisine of Japan is based on rice with miso soup and other dishes. There is an emphasis on seasonal ingredients. Side dishes often consist of fish, pickled vegetables, and vegetables cooked in broth. Seafood is common, often grilled, but also served raw as sashimi or in sushi. Seafood and vegetables are also deep-fried in a light batter, as tempura.

Apart from rice, staples include noodles, such as soba and udon. Japan has many simmered dishes such as fish products in broth called oden, or beef in sukiyaki and nikujaga. Historically, the Japanese shunned meat, but with the modernization of Japan in the 1880s, meat-based dishes such as tonkatsu became common.

Japanese cuisine, particularly sushi, has become popular throughout the world. As of 2011, Japan overtook France in number of Michelin-starred restaurants and has maintained the title since.

Supearibu no Nikomi (Braised Spare Ribs)

Serves 4

Ingredients:
4 pounds pork ribs
½ teaspoon salt
½ teaspoon ground black pepper.
2 tablespoons peanut oil

BBQ Sauce:
1 cup brown sugar
1 cup soy sauce
¼ cup rice wine
½ cup water
1 small onion finally chopped
1 small pear, peeled and finally grated
3 tablespoons crushed garlic
1 tablespoon dark sesame oil
¼ teaspoon ground black pepper
½ teaspoon crushed hot red pepper flakes

This is probably the best homemade BBQ ribs ever, no exaggeration. I've never met anyone who didn't like it. It is simple, delicious, and spicy. This is one of those dishes that will keep people coming back for more! I know that your family will love this never-fail recipe for fall off the bone ribs. You will braise the ribs on each side first. This will give you restaurant-quality results from a home kitchen. Braising the ribs before adding them to your crock pot, gives you the best tasting ribs.

1. Heat oil in large skillet over medium heat.
2. Season the ribs on both sides with salt and pepper. Brown the ribs over medium heat; it should take 3 to 4 minutes per side.
3. Add each rib to your crockpot as they finish browning.
4. In a bowl, mix together the bbq sauce.
5. Pour sauce over ribs, and turn to coat.
6. Cover with lid and cook 3 hours on high or 6 hours on low.

Cabbage Stew

Serves 6

Ingredients:
Nonstick cooking spray
6 cups packaged shredded coleslaw mix
1 ¼ pounds ground pork
1 cup chopped bok choy leaves or fresh spinach
2 small red bell peppers, chopped
1 medium onion, chopped
2 carrots, peeled and sliced
1 stalk celery, chopped
2 green onions chopped
½ teaspoon salt
¼ teaspoon ground black pepper
2 tablespoons red miso (bean paste)
4 cups chicken broth
¼ cup soy sauce
3 tablespoons tomato paste
2 tablespoons sherry wine
1 tablespoon rice vinegar
¼ teaspoon dried thyme

Remember the cabbage soup diet? It was a quick fix solution and considered by many to be a bit of a miracle that can help people lose up to 10 pounds in a single week. This cabbage stew is rumored, in days of old, to be the Japanese recipe to melt away those pounds. It's definitely a go to recipe when you're trying to lose some weight. This wonderful stew is easy, delicious, and healthy.

1. Lightly coat crock pot with cooking spray.
2. In a large bowl combine coleslaw mix, raw ground pork, bok choy, red peppers, onion, celery, green onions, salt, black pepper, and red miso. Place mixture in crock pot.
3. In a medium bowl whisk together chicken broth, soy sauce, tomato paste, sherry, rice vinegar, and thyme.
4. Pour broth mixture over pork mixture in crock pot; stir to combine.
5. Cover with lid and cook 4 hours on high or 8 hours on low. Eat this stew whenever you feel hungry.

People claim you can drop 10 pounds or more in a week. Some people use it to kick-start their weight loss plan, or to trim a few pounds for a special event. But before you stock up on cabbage, know that this crash diet won't help you in the long run, and it doesn't give your body the nutrients it needs to stay healthy.

Beef Sukiyaki

Serves 4

Ingredients:
1 ½ pounds steak, trimmed of fat, sliced very thin
10 scallions including green tops, cut diagonally into 1-inch lengths
1 cup chicken broth
⅔ cup soy sauce
⅓ cup sake or dry white wine
¼ cup sugar
½ pound Napa cabbage, cut into 1-inch pieces
8-ounces shirataki noodles

Sukiyaki is one of the most popular hot pot dishes in Japan. It has a sweet and salty flavor a little bit like teriyaki sauce, but with beef and vegetables in the mix, it has its own Sukiyaki taste people love so much. Although Sukiyaki is a Japanese "national" food like sushi, it is different by region. This recipe is fantastic, so tender, and just yummy!

1. Mix all ingredients in crock pot EXCEPT noodles.
2. Cover with lid and cook 4 hours on high or 8 hours on low.
3. Cook noodles as instructed on package.
4. Add noodles to serving bowls and top with beef sukiyaki from crock pot.

Hamburger Steak

Serves 4

Ingredients:
1 package shimeji mushrooms (or mushroom of your choice)
1 onion, sliced

Beef Patties
1 ½ pounds lean ground beef
1 egg yolk
¼ cup minced onion
⅓ cup Panko bread crumbs
3 tablespoons milk
1 clove garlic
1 teaspoon salt
½ teaspoons ground black pepper

Sauce:
1 ½ cups beef broth
1 (.87 oz.) package brown gravy mix
2 tablespoons ketchup
1 teaspoon Dijon

Thickening:
2 tablespoons corn starch

This is a popular Japanese dish, sort of a really tasty take on Salisbury steak. Its quick, cheap, easy and sooo good. Panko bread crumbs are key here. Bring a Japanese steakhouse favorite into the home with this delicious hamburger.

1. Place mushrooms and onions in the bottom of your crock pot
2. Combine beef patty ingredients and form 6 patties. Brown over medium high heat (about 3 minutes per side).
3. Layer cooked beef patties over mushrooms and onions.
4. Combine sauce ingredients and pour our over beef.
5. Cover with lid and cook 3 hours on high or 6 hours on low.
6. Remove beef patties from crock pot.
7. In a cup combine cornstarch with 3 tablespoons of juice from crock pot, mix well. Stir into the crock pot and let cook a few minutes until thickened. Add beef back into the sauce to coat.

Shoyu Chicken

Serves 2

Ingredients:
6 bone-in chicken thighs
1 tablespoon minced garlic
1 ½ tablespoons Worcestershire sauce
1 cup soy sauce
1 cup sugar
3 tablespoons apple cider vinegar
¼ teaspoon ground black pepper
1 teaspoon peeled and crushed fresh
ginger
2 tablespoons cornstarch

One of Hawaii's most popular plate lunch dishes, deliciously showcasing the state's Japanese culture. Shoyu, is a borrowed Japanese word for soy sauce. The shoyu juices and chicken grease are perfect for sopping up with heaps of steaming white rice. You'll wonder how anyone can stop with just one helping, that's why this recipe serves two. Shoyu Chicken is a classic Hawaiian dish that is everyone's local favorite!

1. Mix all ingredients in crock pot EXCEPT cornstarch
2. Cover with lid and cook 3 hours on high or 6 hours on low.
3. Remove chicken to serving dishes.
4. In a cup, add cornstarch with 3 tablespoons of liquid form the crock pot, stir until smooth and then mix into the crock pot.
5. Pour sauce from crock pot over chicken and serve.

MEXICAN

Gumbo page 94

Mexican cuisine is primarily a fusion of cooking with European, especially Spanish, elements added. The staples are native foods, such as corn, beans, avocados, tomatoes, and chili peppers, along with rice, which was brought by the Spanish. Europeans introduced many other foods, the most important of which were meats from domesticated animals (beef, pork, chicken, goat, and sheep), dairy products (especially cheese), and various herbs and spices.

While the Spanish initially tried to impose their own diet on the country, this was not possible and eventually the foods and cooking techniques began to be mixed. African influences were also introduced into the mixture during this era as a result of African slavery in New Spain.

Over the centuries, this resulted in regional cuisines based on local conditions, such as those in Oaxaca, Veracruz and the Yucatán Peninsula. Mexican cuisine is an important aspect of the culture, social structure, and popular traditions of Mexico. The most important example of this connection is the use of mole for special occasions and holidays, particularly in the South and Center regions of the country.

Taco Soup

Serves 4

Ingredients:
1 pound ground beef
2 medium onions, diced
1 can black beans (with liquid)
1 can red kidney beans (with liquid)
2 cups water
1 can whole kernel corn, drained
1 can diced tomatoes (with liquid)
2 cans diced green chilies
1 (1 ¼ oz.) package taco seasoning mix
1 (1 oz.) package ranch salad dressing mix
Sour cream and cilantro for garnish

This soup is composed of similar ingredients to those used inside a taco. It's a warming dish on a cold day. And since it uses packaged seasonings and several cans of vegetables it's delicious and quick. Get a little heat and a lot of flavor with this taco soup.

1. Brown the ground beef, drain the excess fat, and then transfer the browned beef to crock pot.
2. Add the onions, beans, water, corn, tomatoes, green chilies, taco seasoning, and ranch dressing mix to the crock pot and mix everything together.
3. Cover with lid and cook 4 hours on high or 8 hours on low.

Top with sour cream and cilantro.

Chorizo Cheesy Potatoes

Serves 4

Ingredients:
3 russet potatoes, peeled and diced
1 jar of your favorite salsa
1 link chorizo, sliced
1 ½ cups shredded cheddar cheese
½ cup sour cream
¼ teaspoon dried oregano
¼ teaspoon dried basil
1 (10.75-ounce) can condensed cream of chicken soup
½ teaspoon salt
½ teaspoon ground black pepper
Chopped fresh parsley leaves

It is hard to resist this creamy, cheesy chorizo and potato casserole. Easily made right in your crockpot. A time-tested, delicious combination that everyone loves. This cheesy, creamy one-pot meal that's so creamy and cheesy it will have them coming back for seconds!

1. Mix all ingredients in crock pot.
2. Cover with lid and cook 3 hours on high or 6 hours on low.

Serve immediately, garnished with parsley

Chili Cheese Dip

Serves 6

Ingredients:
1 pound ground beef
1 jar of chunky salsa
1 can kidney beans, rinsed and drained
1 can black beans, rinsed and drained
1 can (14 ½ oz.) diced tomatoes with liquid
1 cup frozen corn
¾ cup water
1 can (2 ¼ oz.) sliced black olives, drained
1 tablespoon chili powder
1 teaspoon hot pepper sauce
¼ teaspoon garlic powder
½ teaspoon ground cumin
1 package (16 oz.) Velveeta cheese, cubed

Crock Pot Chili Cheese Dip is so easy to throw together and the perfect dip for your next party. This meaty, creamy, lightened up Chili Cheese Dip with Velveeta cheese is perfect party food!

1. In a large skillet, cook beef over medium heat, 10 minutes, breaking up beef into crumbles, drain.
2. Transfer to a crock pot.
3. Stir in Velveeta cheese, salsa, beans, tomatoes, corn, water, olives, chili powder, hot pepper sauce, garlic powder and cumin.
4. Cover with lid and cook on high 2 hours, stirring occasional till cheese is melted.

Serve with your favorite nacho chips.

Chicken Mole

Serves 4

Ingredients:
8 skinless boneless chicken thighs
3 cups chicken broth
2 cups orange juice
2 onions, sliced
½ cup sliced almonds
2 tablespoon minced garlic
1 teaspoon cumin
1 teaspoon coriander
1 (4 oz.) can diced green Chiles
¼ cup raisins
½ teaspoons dried oregano
1 tablespoon cocoa powder
1 teaspoon sugar

Garnish:
Sesame seeds

Rich, dark and delicious, mole is a signature sauce in Mexican cooking. Chocolate and spices add richness to the Mexican chile sauce called mole (MOH-lay). An effortless recipe, made in a crock pot.

1. Mix all ingredients in crock pot.
2. Cover with lid and cook 3 hours on high or 6 hours on low.
3. Using tongs, transfer chicken to large serving dish.
4. Working in small batches, transfer sauce mixture from crock pot to blender and puree until smooth; pour over chicken.

Sprinkle with sesame seeds. Serve with rice and warm tortillas.

Extra mole sauce can be kept chilled in your refrigerator. Rewarm over low heat and serve with another meal like grilled chicken.

Gumbo

Serves 4

Ingredients:
2 boneless chicken breast cut into large chunks
½ teaspoon ground black pepper
¼ teaspoon cayenne pepper
1 pound smoked sausage, cut into ¼ inch slices
3 tablespoons butter
1 large onion, chopped
2 tablespoons minced garlic
1 green bell pepper, seeded and chopped
3 stalks celery chopped
¼ cup Worcestershire sauce
4 cups hot water
5 beef bouillon cubes
1 (14-ounce can) stewed tomatoes with juice
2 cups frozen or fresh sliced okra
½ -pound small shrimp, peeled, deveined
2 tablespoons cornstarch

Of all the dishes in the realm of Louisiana cooking, gumbo is the most famous and, very likely, the most popular. Although ingredients might vary greatly from one Mexican chef to the next, and from one part of the state to another, a steaming bowl of fragrant gumbo is one of life's cherished pleasures.

In the mid-19th century, gumbo shifted from being a dish associated with the West Indies to one associated with New Orleans, perhaps thanks to the extent to which cooks and diners of all races had embraced it in Louisiana.

1. Add all ingredients to your crock pot EXCEPT shrimp and cornstarch and mix well.
2. Cover with lid and cook 3 hours on high or 6 hours on low.
3. Add shrimp, cover, and cook on high for an additional thirty minutes.
4. In a cup, add cornstarch with 3 tablespoons of liquid form the crock pot, stir until smooth and then mix into the crock pot.
5. Cover and cook on high for another 30 minutes.

PORTUGUESE

Carne de Porco Alentejana (Pork and Clams) page 100

Portuguese cuisine is born from the earth. It is hearty fare full of strong flavors, many charting the culinary history of the country. For instance, the famous dried salt cod or bacalhau changed the course of Portuguese history. When it was discovered that the beautiful white fish caught in the cold Scandinavian waters could be dried and kept for extended periods, sailors could go on long voyages of discovery to new lands, which then opened trade routes. So, loved is bacalhau now that there are recipe books entirely devoted to it, with a range of recipes from around the country.

Paprika, bay leaves, garlic, and wine are feature largely in many dishes. Olive oil is adored and used to make both recipes and to finish off dishes. Pork is a favorite meat and is used in the famous chouriço sausage, which is smoked over wood with heady aromas of garlic and paprika.

Desserts rely heavily on eggs – think crème caramel, rice pudding and the famous custard tarts or pasteis de nata. A selection of cheeses may also be served, with the most common varieties being made from sheep or goat's milk.

Stone Soup

Serves 4

Ingredients:
3 cans red kidney beans with juices from cans
1 link of chouriço sausage, sliced
1 large onion, chopped
2 carrots peeled and chopped
1 tablespoon minced garlic
¼ cup bacon fat (cook up a pound of bacon and save the fat)
1 (6 ounce) can tomato paste
1 cup tomato puree
4 cups water
1 bay leaf
1 tablespoon paprika
½ teaspoon tabasco sauce
1 ½ teaspoon salt
½ teaspoon ground black pepper

The soup gets its name from the kidney beans, which are referred to as "stones". Legend has it that a hungry friar begging for food knocked at the door of a farm laborer's house. When the laborer tried to turn him away, the friar picked up stones and asked him to lend him a pot and some water so that he could make a delicious stone soup. The laborer and his family agreed. As the water boiled, the friar remarked that the soup would improve considerably if they gave him some lard. Tasting the soup at various intervals, the friar asked for and obtained salt and some smoked sausage. When he had eaten it, only the stones remained at the bottom of the pot. Questioned by the family over what he would do with the stones, the friar replied that he would rinse and let dry and take it with him for use the next time he was hungry.

1. Add and mix everything together in crock pot.
2. Cover with lid and cook 4 hours on high or 8 hours on low

Favas Stew

Serves 4

Ingredients:
1 tablespoon olive oil
3 large onions – sliced and cut in quarters
1 tablespoon crushed garlic
1 ½ cups of water
½ teaspoon of crushed red hot pepper flakes
8 oz. can tomato sauce
½ tablespoon of dried parsley
½ teaspoon of black pepper
1 tablespoon of paprika
1 teaspoons salt
1 link of chouriço sausage, sliced
2 cans fava beans, like Progresso

I've had many requests for this recipe. Most of them have been from people who has eaten this dish at Portuguese festivals and want to make it at home. Fava beans slow simmered in a juicy sauce with onions and Portuguese sausage. Try this juicy, spicy, and delicious dish.

1. Add all ingredients to your crock pot and mix together.
2. Cover with lid and cook 4 hours on high or 8 hours on low.

Sausage Stew

Serves 4

Ingredients:
2 links of chouriço sausage, sliced
1 large red onion, sliced and cut into quarters
½ pound fresh string beans
3 carrots, peeled and sliced
1 red bell pepper, sliced
1 can great northern beans, navy, or pinto with liquid
1 (28 oz.) can crushed tomatoes
1 teaspoon salt
2 teaspoons minced garlic
1 teaspoon paprika
½ teaspoon ground black pepper
¼ teaspoon hot crushed red pepper
2 cups vegetable stock
Fresh parsley for garnish

A delicious hearty stew. I always loved Portuguese style stews. I think this version makes a great dish. Make sure you have plenty of crusty bread for dipping in the sauce!

1. Add all ingredients to your crock pot and mix together.
2. Cover with lid and cook 4 hours on high or 8 hours on low.

Sausage, Chicken and Potatoes

Serves 4

Ingredients:
6 chicken thighs, bone-in
2 teaspoons paprika
2 links of chouriço sausage,
sliced
5 potatoes, quartered
1 tablespoon minced garlic
1 large bay leaf
½ teaspoon hot crushed red
pepper
1 onion, chopped
⅓ cup sherry wine
1 cup chicken stock
1 teaspoon grated lemon zest
1 teaspoon grated orange zest
2 cups crushed tomatoes
1 teaspoon dried parsley

Garnish:
Black olives and parsley

The all-time favorite; is simple to prepare and comes out perfect every time. Every home cook can make this chicken practically with their eyes closed and each family has their own recipe. This dish will leave you speechless!

1. Add and mix everything together in crock pot.
2. Cover with lid and cook 4 hours on high or 8 hours on low.

Garnish with black olives and parsley.

Carne de Porco Alentejana (Pork and Clams)

Serves 4

Ingredients
2 ½ - 3 pounds boneless pork loin, cut into 1 inch cubes
1 large onion, chopped
1 teaspoon sugar
2 tablespoon tomato paste mixed with ½ cup water
1 tsp dried parsley
1 teaspoon paprika
1 ½ cups dry white wine
¼ teaspoon black pepper
2 teaspoons salt
¼ teaspoon onion powder
1 large bay leaf
1 tablespoon crushed garlic
24 fresh uncooked little neck clams, rinsed, allow to rest at room temperature

This is one of the most traditional and popular pork and seafood dishes of Portuguese cuisine. It is typical from the Alentejo region, in Portugal, hence the word Alentejana in its name. This dish relies on wine and garlic and creates a delicious sauce. Try this easy crock pot recipe. Do not be intimidated! Cooking clams in the crockpot is easier than it seems.

1. Add and mix all the ingredients to crock pot EXCEPT clams.
2. Cover with lid and cook 3 hours on high or 6 hours on low.
3. Mix clams into crock pot and cook an additional hour on high.

Within an hour, you will see the clams open and soak themselves in this delicious broth. This is an unbelievable way to cook your clams in a crock pot.

Alcatra (Shredded Beef)

Serves 6

Ingredients:
2 pounds beef

Marinade:
¼ cup white wine
¼ cup red wine
½ cup beef stock
½ cup tomato sauce
2 tablespoons red wine vinegar
2 tablespoons dark brown sugar
1 teaspoon minced garlic
1 tablespoon dry granulated onion
1 teaspoon salt
1 teaspoon cumin
1 teaspoon ground black pepper
2 teaspoons paprika
½ teaspoon coriander
¼ teaspoon nutmeg
½ teaspoon all spice
⅛ teaspoon clove
1 bay leaf

This meaty, clean-tasting Portuguese version of beef stew, called alcatra, requires mere minutes of hands-on work. Alcatra is a pot roast very popular in the Azorean Island of Terceira in Portugal. Terceira is one of the nine Islands of the Azores. It's the Island with the second largest population of the Azores. This is a traditional Portuguese slow cooker pot roast and is probably the most widely eaten simply because of how good it tastes. This slow cooked meal has an amazing smell in the house which makes people gravitate towards the kitchen. The meat becomes incredibly tender, the sauce is rich and the flavor is amazing! This recipe can easily be doubled for pot-luck gatherings.

1. In a large bowl mix marinade ingredients together. Add beef and refrigerate for 24 hours.
2. Add meat with marinate into your crock pot. My crock pot has an inner pot that comes out. I marinate the meat inside the pot and refrigerate. Take it out the next day and just put it back into my crock pot.
3. Cover with lid and cook 4 hours on high or 8 hours on low.

Bread Pudding

Serves 6

Ingredients:
1 loaf Portuguese sweet bread (8 cups, cubed 1-inch pieces)
½ cup water
½ cup granulated sugar
2 teaspoons vanilla extract
1 tablespoon ground cinnamon
1 ½ cups whole milk
½ cup heavy cream
5 large eggs

Topping:
Caramel sauce
Pecan brittle
Vanilla ice cream

This is a simple and easy to make delicious Portuguese bread pudding.

1. Generously spray your crockpot with nonstick cooking spray.
2. In a small saucepan, add the water, and sugar. Bring the mixture to a boil over medium high heat, stirring until the sugar dissolves. Once boiling, remove from the heat. Stir in the vanilla extract and cinnamon. Set aside and let cool for about 15 minutes.
3. In a large bowl, add the milk, cream, and eggs. Whisk until well combined. Add in the cooled sugar mixture, whisking to combine.
4. Add in the bread cubes and mix until all the bread is coated with the mixture.
5. Transfer the mixture to your crockpot.
6. Cover and cook on low for about 2 hours or until set.

To serve – scoop the bread pudding into bowls, and add a generous amount of the toppings.

SPANISH

Almejas Con Chorizo (Clams & Sausage) page 110

It would be impossible to list all the tasty foods from the rich Spanish food culture – but here are some of my favorites. Spanish recipes you just have to try. While Spain's tapas are a gourmet exploration, here are some more top Spanish foods you will make repeatedly.

Spanish food is often recognized as one of the top cuisines in the world, and some traditional Spanish dishes and recipes date hundreds of years. Food has become as integral to Spain as its rich and tumultuous history, with each region of Spain – once a collection of numerous, distinct kingdoms – boasting their own unique cuisines and flavors.

Each regional specialty in Spain is worth trying, and many of the top Spanish restaurants are known by the different regions they come from.

Chili

Serves 6

Ingredients:
1 pound ground beef
2 tablespoons olive oil
1 large red onion, diced
1 medium red bell pepper, diced
1 medium yellow bell pepper, diced
1 tablespoon minced garlic
½ pound ground Chorizo sausage
¼ cup chili powder
1 tablespoon ground cumin
1 teaspoon dried oregano
1 teaspoon salt
4 ounces can tomato paste mixed
with 1 cup water
12-ounce bottle Spain Estrella beer
of other pale lager
28 ounces can tomato, crushed
15 ounces can black beans, with
liquid
15 ounces can dark red kidney
beans, with liquid
15 ounces can pinto beans, with
liquid

The secret to this wholesome, hearty chili recipe is bright, plump, tender 3 bean combos, red, black and pinto. The beans simmer gently in tomato with ground beef and chorizo, they soak up the robust seasonings for a meaty, savory bean chili that's a delicious one-pot meal, any day of the week.

While Mexican chorizo is seasoned with chili peppers and vinegar, Spanish chorizo is made basically with pork, sweet paprika and garlic.

1. Brown ground beef in olive oil till it's no longer pink, drain and add to crockpot.
2. Add all other ingredients and mix well.
3. Cover with lid and cook 4 hours on high or 8 hours on low.

Garnish with cheese, green onions, and parsley, optional

Patatas Bravas (Chicken, Sausage & Potatoes)

Serves 4

Ingredients:
2 pounds boneless chicken sliced into ½ inch strips
½ pound new potatoes sliced in half
1 link chorizo, sliced
1 pound cherry tomatoes, sliced in half
2 teaspoons minced garlic
1 onion finely chopped
2 teaspoons of paprika
¼ teaspoon cayenne pepper
1 teaspoon sherry vinegar
1 teaspoon sugar
1 teaspoon salt
½ teaspoon ground black pepper

Garnish:
Chopped flat leaf parsley

Patatas bravas is a dish native to Spain, often served in restaurants and tapa bars throughout the country. It typically consists of white potatoes in a spicy tomato sauce.

Spanish tapas are tasty small plates that when combined create a light supper or great appetizer. As with most tapas, each bar and household will have its own recipe, naturally believed to the best! Savor this mildly tangy version with chicken and chorizo. The result is incredibly delicious!

1. Add all ingredients to your crock pot and mix well.
2. Cover with lid and cook 4 hours on high or 8 hours on low.

Garnish with parsley.

Spicy Baked Beans

Serves 6

Ingredients:
1 package hot dogs, sliced into bite size pieces
1 package chorizo, sliced
2 medium onions, chopped
3 teaspoons crushed garlic
1 tablespoon spicy brown mustard
2 tablespoons Worcestershire sauce
1 tablespoon soy sauce
1 tablespoon Frank's Red Hot sauce
¼ cup of ketchup
¼ cup dark brown sugar
½ cup dry red wine
2 (15oz) cans of B&M Original Baked Beans
5 slices smoked bacon, cooked and crumbled

What's better than bacon, sausage, and hot dogs. Have it as a main dish or side dish. This one is not to be missed.

1. Mix all ingredients in crock pot.
2. Cover with lid and cook 3 hours on high or 6 hours on low.

Spicy Orange Pork

Serves 6

Ingredients:
2 pound pork (tenderloin, boneless pork chops, or boneless ribs)
1 teaspoon ground cumin
2 tablespoons sugar
1 teaspoon ground coriander
2 teaspoons salt
½ teaspoon ground pepper
4 jalapeño chilies, seeded and finely chopped
2 tablespoons minced garlic
¼ teaspoon dried oregano
3 tablespoons sherry wine
1 cup orange juice

A delicious flavored Spanish recipe with orange juice, herbs, plenty of garlic and some jalapeños, deliver enough flavor to satisfy your spicy craving.

1. Mix all ingredients in crock pot.
2. Cover with lid and cook 4 hours on high or 8 hours on low.

Braised Pork Chops

Serves 4

Ingredients:
4 bone-in pork chops
2 tablespoons oil
1 tablespoon sugar

Marinade:
3 tablespoons minced garlic
1 teaspoon salt
½ teaspoon ground black pepper
1 onion chopped, finely
1 jalapeño pepper, seeded, cored, and diced
¼ teaspoon dried oregano
¾ teaspoons cumin
¾ cup Goya bitter orange marinade
1 lime, juiced
½ cup white wine
½ cup chicken stock

Experience the tantalizing taste of this dish. A delicious dish that is part of the rich culinary tradition in Spain.

1. Mix all marinade ingredients together. Add the pork and marinate overnight.
2. Next day - Heat the oil in a skillet over medium high heat.
3. Brown the pork and brown in small batches, approximately 2 minutes per side. (be sure to save the marinade)
4. Add the browned meat to your crock pot as each piece is browned.
5. When all the meat is browned add the saved marinate to the pan to deglaze the pan, stirring constantly for a few minutes.
6. Add the marinade from the pan to your crock pot over the pork chops.
7. Add the sugar.
8. Cover with lid and cook 3 hours on high or 6 hours on low.

Ropa Vieja Chicken

Serves 6

Ingredients:
2 pounds boneless chicken cut up into 2 inch pieces
1 ½ teaspoons salt
½ teaspoon ground black pepper
1 Cubanelle pepper or green bell pepper, seeded and diced
1 red bell pepper, seeded and diced
1 onion, diced
1 tablespoon minced garlic
½ cup white wine
1 (28 oz.) can crushed tomato
2 tablespoons tomato paste
1 cup chicken broth
1 teaspoon ground cumin
½ teaspoon dried oregano
1 bay leaf
1 tablespoon white vinegar

Ropa Vieja means "old clothes" in Spanish. Old clothes tend to be shredded and so is the chicken in this dish.

1. Mix all ingredients in crock pot.
2. Cover with lid and cook 4 hours on high or 8 hours on low.
3. One finished cooking take 2 forks and shred chicken.

Serve as a meal with rice or makes great sandwiches.

Almejas Con Chorizo (Clams & Sausage)

Serves 4

Ingredients:
24 fresh uncooked little neck clams, rinsed, allow to rest at room temperature
2 links of chorizo, sliced
2 cups tomato sauce
1 large onion, sliced
½ cup of hot pepper rings from a jar
1 ½ cup dry white wine
3 tablespoons minced garlic
⅛ teaspoon dried thyme
1 ½ teaspoons salt
½ teaspoon black ground pepper
1 teaspoons sugar
1 bay leaf
2 tablespoons tomato paste
1 tablespoon olive oil
2 envelope packets Sazon Goya (Con Azafran)

Do not be intimidated! Cooking clams is easier than it seems. This recipe is prepared with tomato sauce, white wine and sausage that give a great flavor. An excellent hot and spicy dish served with lightly toasted roll, so that you can soak in this delicious sauce. You can also use for Spanish tapas.

1. Add all ingredients to the crock pot EXCEPT the littleneck clams.
2. Cover with lid and cook 3 hours on high or 6 hours on low.
3. Add clams and cook on high for an additional hour.

Serve with some crusty fresh bread.

THAI

Massaman Curry page 118

Thai cuisine is the national cuisine of Thailand. Balance, detail, and variety are of paramount significance to Thai chefs.

Thai cooking places emphasis on lightly prepared dishes with strong aromatic components and a spicy edge. It is known for its complex interplay of at least three and up to four or five fundamental taste senses in each dish or the overall meal: sour, sweet, salty, bitter, and spicy. Thai cooking rejects simplicity and is about juggling elements to create a harmonious finish. Thai foods attention to detail; texture; color; taste; and the use of ingredients with medicinal benefits, as well as good flavor, gives the food's appearance, smell, and context.

Thai cuisine is one of the most popular cuisines in the world. In 2011, seven of Thailand's popular dishes appeared on the list of the "World's 50 Most Delicious Foods" a worldwide online poll of 35,000 people by CNN Travel. Thailand had more dishes on the list than any other country. They were: tom yum goong (4th), pad Thai (5th), som tam (6th), massaman curry (10th), green curry (19th), Thai fried rice (24th) and moo nam tok (36th).

Tom Yum Goong (Shrimp Soup)

Serves 4

Ingredients:
6 cups of water
¼ cup lemongrass, sliced
1 inch chunk of galangal, ground
2 teaspoons Sambal Oelek (chili paste)
2 tablespoons minced garlic
½ pound of oyster mushrooms
1 tablespoon tomato paste
2 onions, chopped
1 teaspoon salt
2 teaspoons of sugar
4 tablespoons of fish sauce
2 tablespoons of lime juice
1 pound large shrimp, devein and shell removed
Handful of fresh cilantro

One of the most famous of all Thai foods, and what I think is one the best soups in the world. What I love most about this soup is the flavors of lemongrass, galangal, lime juice, that all combine to create a healthy and soothing broth that will light up your taste buds. If you're looking to cook an awesome and authentic soup, try this tom yum soup recipe. This recipe is for local Thai street food style tom yum soup – it's not the fancy kind – but follow this recipe for the authentic taste you'll find in Thailand.

1. Mix all ingredients in crock pot EXCEPT shrimp.
2. Cover with lid and cook 3 hours on high or 6 hours on low.
3. Mix in shrimp and cook on high an additional hour.

Garnish with fresh cilantro.

Coconut Shrimp Soup

Serves 6

Ingredients:
2 tablespoons grated fresh ginger
1 stalk lemon grass, minced
2 teaspoons red curry paste
5 cups chicken broth
½ cup long grain white rice, uncooked
3 tablespoons fish sauce
1 tablespoon light brown sugar
1 can coconut milk
2 tablespoons butter
½ pound shiitake mushrooms, sliced
2 tablespoons fresh lime juice
½ teaspoon salt
½ teaspoon ground black pepper
1 pound medium shrimp - peeled and deveined

Bold, and delicious Thai flavors make this soup irresistible! This is the best Thai coconut soup I've had. You won't be disappointed with this one!

1. Add and mix everything together in crock pot EXCEPT shrimp.
2. Cover with lid and cook 2 hours on high or 4 hours on low.
3. Mix in shrimp and cook on high an additional hour.

Garnish with fresh cilantro.

Chicken Wings

Serves 4

Ingredients:
15-20 chicken wings

Sauce:
1 ½ tablespoon Sambal, or another Asian-style chili paste.
¾ cup apricot preserve
1 cup water
⅓ cup rice vinegar
2 teaspoons minced garlic
½ teaspoon sesame oil
¼ cup hoisin sauce
⅓ cup sugar
1 teaspoon granular chicken bouillon

Garnish – green onion, sliced

These easy, spicy chicken wings are an excellent alternative to regular hot wings! I learned this recipe from a friend from Taiwan, and it was always a favorite! Almost all seasonings can be adjusted according to taste. The Asian-style chili paste can be found at any oriental grocery or even most regular groceries in the Asian section.

1. Place Chicken wings in crock pot.
2. Combine all sauce ingredients and blend together well and pour over chicken wings, mix in.
3. Cover with lid and cook 3 hours on high or 6 hours on low.
4. Remove wings carefully to a greased cookie sheet, as the wings will be very tender.
5. Baste wings with a little more sauce from crock pot.
6. Broil in oven for 5-10 minutes and baste wings again before serving.

Curry Ground Beef

Serves 4

Ingredients:
1 pound lean ground beef
1 tablespoon olive oil
1 cup thinly sliced green onions
1 teaspoon minced garlic
2 teaspoons red curry paste
1 cup tomato sauce
½ cup coconut milk
½ cup water
1 tablespoon brown sugar
¼ teaspoon lime zest
1 ½ teaspoons fresh lime juice
1 tablespoon fish sauce

Thai cooking places emphasis on lightly prepared dishes with strong aromatic components and a spicy edge. This is a wonderful recipe. A delicious way to use ground beef. You can make it spicier by using more red curry paste.

1. Add oil to a pan and heat over medium high heat.
2. Add ground beef and brown till no longer pink, drain.
3. Add cooked ground beef and all other ingredients to your crock pot and mix together.
4. Cover with lid and cook 3 hours on high or 6 hours on low.

Serve with white rice.

Drunken Noodles

Serves 4

Ingredients:
1 ½ pounds boneless chicken cut
into bite size pieces
1 onion, sliced
2 tablespoons chopped garlic
1 tablespoons fish sauce
2 tablespoon soy sauce
1 tablespoon oyster sauce
2 tablespoons chili sauce
1 teaspoon chili paste
1 teaspoon sugar
½ cup tomato puree
2 cups chicken stock
2 cups water
½ cup chopped fresh basil
2 jalapeno peppers (seeds removed,
sliced)
1 package fresh Fettuccine noodles
(8oz – ½ pound) Cut in half if
needed to fit inside your crock pot.
Usually found in the produce area
of your supermarket.

There is no alcohol in the ingredients, so why "drunken"? Well, you must understand the different drinking habits in Thailand. The Thais do not drink before meals like Westerners. They have a meal while they are drinking. In general, they don't drink without food. Someone under the influence of alcohol, their taste buds are impaired due to the alcohol. So, the food that they would like to eat usually has much more intense taste, saltier and spicier. "Drunken Noodles" is the ultimate example. Yes, there is alcohol in the mix; you just have to drink it on the side.

1. Place all ingredients in the crock pot EXCEPT basil, jalapeno peppers and noodles.
2. Cover with lid and cook 3 hours on high or 6 hours on low.
3. Mix in basil, jalapeno peppers and noodles cook on high for an additional hour. Stir occasionally so noodles don't stick together.

Spicy Chicken Stew

Serves 6

Ingredients:
2 pounds boneless chicken cut
into bite size pieces.
1 small red bell pepper, seeded,
cored cut into 1 inch chunks
1 jalapeño pepper, seeded, cored,
and chopped
2 carrots, sliced
4 potatoes peeled and cut into
quarters
1 onion, sliced
12 grape tomatoes sliced in half
2 teaspoons minced garlic
½ teaspoon dry ginger
1 tablespoon dark brown sugar
1 tablespoon red curry paste
1 tablespoon fish sauce
1 teaspoon salt
½ teaspoon ground black pepper
1 ½ teaspoons fresh lime juice
One 14-ounce can unsweetened
coconut milk
1 cup chicken stock

The Thai accents in this fragrant chicken stew come from creamy coconut milk, ginger, salty fish sauce and lime. Asian flavorings can provide so many wonderful additions to rather ordinary foods. This Thai chicken stew is spicy and tastes delicious.

1. Add and mix everything together in crock pot.
2. Cover with lid and cook 4 hours on high or 8 hours on low.

Massaman Curry

Serves 4

Ingredients:
1 pound beef stew meat
1 cinnamon stick
1 cup beef broth
½ cup coconut milk
2 teaspoons masaman curry paste or if you can't find, use red curry paste
1 cup onion, chopped
2 potatoes, peeled cut into quarters
1 tablespoon fish sauce
1 teaspoon salt
2 tablespoons sugar
2 teaspoons tamarind soup mix
2 bay leaves
¼ cup peanuts

Massaman curry is a rich Thai curry dish that is an interpretation of a Persian dish. Slow-cooked, meltingly tender beef with crunchy peanuts to finish - it's curry heaven.

1. Add and mix everything together in crock pot EXCEPT peanuts.
2. Cover with lid and cook 3 hours on high or 6 hours on low.
3. Remove bay leaves and stir in peanuts and serve.

VIETNAMESE

Banh Mi Thit (Pork Sandwich) page 122

Vietnamese cuisine encompasses the foods and beverages of Vietnam, and features a combination of five fundamental tastes in the overall meal. Each Vietnamese dish has a distinctive flavor which reflects one or more of these elements.

Common ingredients include fish sauce, shrimp paste, soy sauce, rice, fresh herbs, fruit, and vegetables. Vietnamese recipes use lemongrass, ginger, mint, coriander, cinnamon, chili, lime, and Thai basil leaves.

Traditional Vietnamese cooking is greatly admired for its fresh ingredients, minimal use of dairy and oil, complementary textures, and reliance on herbs and vegetables. With the balance between fresh herbs and meats and a selective use of spices to reach a fine taste, Vietnamese food is considered one of the healthiest cuisines worldwide.

Pho (Beef Noodle Soup)

Serves 6

Ingredients:
6 cups beef broth
1 onion, sliced
2 slices fresh ginger root
1 pod star anise
2 tablespoons fish sauce
¾ cup bean sprouts
¼ cup hoisin sauce
1 tablespoon Chile-garlic sauce
(such as Sriracha)
1 package (8 oz.) dried rice
noodles
1 pound flank steak, thinly sliced

Garnish:
¼ cup chopped fresh cilantro
¼ cup chopped fresh basil
green onions, sliced

Making your own fabulous bowl of Vietnamese pho soup at home is not hard and very delicious. This is a wonderfully delicate soup, made with beef, ginger, onions, and lots of aromatic spices. It's nothing short of soup perfection. This soup recipe is made easy. It's cooked with beef broth instead of the beef bones and the beef is not rare like in some recipes.

1. Add and mix everything together in crock pot EXCEPT noodles and steak.
2. Cover with lid and cook 3 hours on high or 6 hours on low.
3. Add steak to crock pot and cook an additional hour on high.
4. Cook noodles to package directions.
5. Divide noodles among serving bowls; top with soup.

Garnish with cilantro, basil, and green onion.

Canh Ga Nuong (Barbecued Chicken Wings)

Serves 4

Ingredients:
15-24 chicken wings

BBQ Sauce:
¾ cup chicken broth
¼ cup honey
2 tablespoons sugar
½ ground black pepper
1 teaspoon garlic powder
2 tablespoons Sriracha Hot Chili sauce
¼ cup soy sauce
1 tablespoon of hoisin sauce
1 tablespoon minced garlic
1 teaspoon white vinegar
½ teaspoon paprika

Sweet and Hot Chicken Wings is a great appetizer for any of your game day parties. It is very easy to make and is much healthier than the deep-fried version. You might want to double this recipe because you're going to wish for more.

1. Place Chicken wings in crock pot.
2. Combine all sauce ingredients and blend together, pour over chicken wings, mix in.
3. Cover with lid and cook 3 hours on high or 6 hours on low.
4. Remove wings carefully to a greased cookie sheet, as the wings will be very tender.
5. Baste wings with a little more sauce from crock pot.
6. Broil in oven for 5-10 minutes and baste wings again before serving.

Banh Mi Thit (Pork Sandwich)

Serves 4

Ingredients:
1 pound boneless pork cut into 2 inch pieces
1 cup beef stock
1 tablespoon rice vinegar
1 teaspoon five-spice powder
1 teaspoon minced garlic
3 tablespoons soy sauce
1 ½ teaspoons sugar
1 tablespoon Sambal chili paste

Serve:
4 French baguettes

Make your very own Vietnamese pork rolls at home with this flavorful recipe, each playing a part in balancing sweet, savory, sour, and spicy. If ever there was a sandwich to launch a thousand ships, banh mi thit, or more simply, banh mi would be it. It's delicious, it's cheap and it has inspired a movement sweeping America.

1. Mix all ingredients in crock pot.
2. Cover with lid and cook 4 hours on high or 8 hours on low.
3. Once finished cooking take 2 forks and shred pork.

Serve as a sandwich with optional garnishes:
Mesclun (is a salad mix of carrots, assorted small, young salad green leaves.
Thai basil
Cilantro leaves
Shallots, sliced
Cucumber, thinly sliced

Suon Heo Kho (Braised Pork Ribs)

Serves 4

Ingredients:
3 to 4 pounds baby back ribs
1 cup beef broth
2 medium shallots, finely chopped
2 tablespoons minced lemon grass
2 tablespoons soy sauce
1 tablespoon fish sauce
1 tablespoon Sambal oelek chile paste
2 teaspoons kosher salt
2 tablespoons brown sugar
2 teaspoons Chinese five-spice powder
1 tablespoon minced garlic
2 tablespoons grated fresh ginger

Caramel flavors and pork are a favorite combination in Vietnam and these caramelized pork spare ribs continue in the tradition. As is signature to Vietnamese fare, the dish is garnished with fresh herbs, which cut through any richness. The ribs are cooked with traditional Vietnamese seasonings, cooked slowly, and browned at the end.

1. Mix all ingredients in crock pot.
2. Cover with lid and cook 3 hours on high or 6 hours on low.
3. Remove ribs carefully to a greased cookie sheet, as the ribs will be very tender.
4. Baste ribs with a little more sauce from crock pot.
5. Broil in oven for 5-10 minutes and baste ribs again before serving.

Garnish with cilantro and mint sprigs.

Caramel Chicken

Serves 4

Ingredients:
⅓ cup brown sugar
½ cup fish sauce
6 bone-in, skin-on chicken thighs
½ medium onion, finely chopped
1 ½ cups chicken broth
1 tablespoon fresh ginger, peeled and finely chopped
2 teaspoons garlic, minced
¼ teaspoon salt
½ teaspoon ground black pepper
½ teaspoon Sambal chili paste

Garnish:
3 green onions, sliced

This Vietnamese caramel chicken is a recipe that is sure to whet your appetite. It's an amazing dish with the simplest ingredients, so easy to make, and it's absolutely delightful.

1. Heat a sauce pan over medium heat. Add sugar and fish sauce cooking until it starts to melt. Reduce heat to medium-low and cook, swirling pan frequently, until caramel is bubbling.
2. Remove pan from heat and pour caramel into a heatproof measuring cup or bowl. Set aside.
3. Place Chicken thighs and onions in crock pot.
4. Mix chicken broth, ginger, garlic, salt, black pepper, and chili paste. Pour over your chicken and onion.
5. Take your caramel sauce and pour over your chicken.
6. Cover crock pot and cook 3 hours on high or 6 hours on low.
7. Remove chicken carefully to a greased cookie sheet, as the chicken thighs will be very tender.
8. Baste chicken with a little more sauce from crock pot.
9. Broil in oven for 5-10 minutes.
10. Baste again before serving and garnish with green onion.

Bo' Kho (Beef Stew)

Serves 4

Ingredients:
2 pounds beef stew meat
½ cup bean sprouts
1 tablespoon minced lemon grass
3 tablespoon fish sauce
1 ½ teaspoon Chinese five spice
1 ½ teaspoons brown sugar
2 ½ tablespoons minced ginger
1 bay leaf
1 onion, chopped
2 cups chopped fresh tomatoes or
1 can crushed tomatoes
½ teaspoon salt
4 carrots, peeled, cut into 1 inch chunks
2 star anise pod
3 cups water

What could be better than eating a bowl of Vietnamese beef stew. Bò Kho blends flavors of earthy spices and popular ingredients from all over Asia. Every time you make this, the whole house smells wonderful.

1. Mix all ingredients in crock pot.
2. Cover with lid and cook 4 hours on high or 8 hours on low.

Serve with optional garnishes:
Thai basil
Cilantro leaves

Thit Bo Luc Lac (Shaking Beef)

Serves 4

Ingredients:
1 pound stew beef meat
1 cup beef stock
2 tablespoons minced garlic
1 tablespoon fish sauce
1 teaspoon sugar
1 teaspoon salt
½ teaspoon ground black pepper
½ teaspoon onion powder
1 tablespoon rice vinegar

Thit bo luc lac, named after the back and forth shaking of the skillet as you sear the cubes of beef, was likely a clever dish invented to deal with tough cuts of steak. This Vietnamese recipe cooks the beef in a crock pot. The result is fork tender meat that pares great with a salad. Great tasting salads are a way to boost your intake of vegetables. ... And, by adding some protein, you can turn that simple salad into a healthy meal.

1. Mix all ingredients in crock pot.
2. Cover with lid and cook 3 hours on high or 6 hours on low.

Specialty Ingredients

Bok Choy - A deep green leafy vegetable that resembles Romaine lettuce on top and a large celery on the bottom, bok choy is a crucifer more closely related to cabbage. The entire vegetable can be used, and is often added raw to salads for a satisfying crunch. Is wildly available in most grocery stores and International aisle of most super markets. Also, available in most local Asian markets.

Chili Sauce - is a condiment prepared with chili peppers and sometimes red tomato as primary ingredients. Is wildly available in most grocery stores and International aisle of most super markets. Also, available in most local Asian markets.

Chili Paste - Cooks can substitute hot sauce or crushed red pepper flakes for chili paste. Chili paste is seasoned with salt and made up of hot peppers, oil, and garlic. Cooks sometimes use dried peppers instead of paste. Is wildly available in most grocery stores and International aisle of most super markets. Also, available in most local Asian markets.

Chinese Cabbage or Napa Cabbage - While several types of Chinese cabbage exist, the variety we most commonly associate with Chinese cabbage is Napa Cabbage, the large-headed cabbage with the firmly packed, pale green leaves that you'll usually find next to bok choy in supermarkets.

Chorizo – is a Spanish sausage and is made from coarsely chopped pork and pork fat, seasoned with pimentón – a smoked paprika – and salt. It is generally classed as either picante (spicy) or dulce (sweet), depending upon the type of pimentón used. Is available in some grocery stores Also, available in most local Spanish markets. Chorizo and Chouriço can be used interchangeably.

Chouriço – is a Portuguese sausage and is made with pork, fat, wine, paprika, garlic, and salt. It is then stuffed into natural or artificial casings and slowly dried over smoke. The many different varieties differ in color, shape, seasoning, and taste. Many dishes of Portuguese cuisine and Brazilian cuisine make use of chouriço. Is available in some grocery stores. Also, available in most local Portuguese markets. Chorizo and Chouriço can be used interchangeably.

Cubanelle Pepper - also known as "Cuban pepper" and "Italian frying pepper", is a variety of sweet pepper of the species Capsicum annuum. When unripe, it is light yellowish-green in color, but will turn bright red if allowed to ripen. If you live outside of areas with Italian or Caribbean influence, they can be hard to find in stores. You substitute bell peppers. You are stepping down to zero heat with this alternative, but the cubanelle is not that far behind. And, of course, the bell pepper is available wherever produce is sold. Both are sweet peppers, so the flavors are in the same ballpark. It's close enough, at least, to substitute when the cubanelle is not an option.

Curry Paste - is a paste used as a cooking ingredient in the preparation of a curry dish. It is an ingredient used in many Indian and Thai dishes. Is wildly available in most grocery stores and International aisle of most super markets. Also, available in most local Asian markets.

Fava Beans - are one of the oldest plants under cultivation, and they were eaten in ancient Greece and Rome. Despite the name, fava beans are a member of the pea family. They are popular in Mediterranean cuisine, with many summer dishes celebrating the seasonal bean, although they are also dried for winter use. Fava beans have a distinct flavor and creamy texture that makes them a great addition to a wide variety of dishes. Is available in some grocery stores where other canned beans are found.

Fermented Black Beans - are not the black beans you find in Latin American cooking; they are actually soybeans - the same as in miso, tofu, and soy sauce. They are an umami powerhouse already - full of that savory, lingering taste that adds depth to any food it touches. Is wildly available in most grocery stores and International aisle of most super markets. Also, available in most local Asian markets.

Fish Sauce - In case you are not yet familiar with fish sauce, it is that salty, smelly brown liquid made from fish that is the single, most important flavoring ingredient in Thai cooking (also well-loved in Laos, Cambodia, Vietnam, Burma and the Philippines). Used like salt in western cooking and soy sauce in Chinese cooking, good-quality fish sauce imparts a distinct aroma and flavor all its own. It is indispensable in the Thai kitchen as Thai food wouldn't be quite the same without it. Is available in some grocery stores and International aisle of some super markets. Also, available in most local Asian markets.

Galangal - (pronounced guh-lang-guh) is often found in Thai, Indonesian, and Malaysian cooking. It's a rhizome - an underground creeping stem of a plant that sends out shooters to create new plants. Ginger is also a rhizome, and at first glance you might mistake galangal for ginger. Galangal is very hard and woody, although the center is usually a little softer and juicier than its woody exterior. Galangal also tastes different than ginger. It's more piney and sharp, with a strong citrus scent. It gives, oddly, both an earthy note and a higher citrus note to curry pastes and dishes. Is available in some grocery stores in the same area as ginger. Also, available in most local Asian markets.

Green Chiles - Named after Puebla, Mexico, this type of pepper has a beautiful dark green color and is wider than the Anaheim chile. It is usually hotter than the Anaheim as well, though its piquancy varies and it can sometimes be very mild. Is wildly available in most grocery stores and International Spanish aisle of most super markets. Also, available in most local Spanish markets.

Goya Mojo Criollo - is a tangy blend of orange and lemon juices, accented with garlic and spices. Marinade in a deep dish, the longer the better, then cook as you usually would. Is wildly available in most grocery stores and International Spanish aisle of most super markets. Also, available in most local Spanish markets.

Goya Adobo All Purpose Seasoning - blends salt, garlic, oregano, and black pepper. It's the classic Puerto Rican seasoning. Is wildly available in most grocery stores and International Spanish aisle of most super markets. Also, available in most local Spanish markets.

Hoisin Sauce - is a thick, pungent sauce commonly used in Chinese cuisine as a glaze for meat, an addition to stir fries, or as dipping sauce. It is darkly colored in appearance and sweet and salty in taste. Is wildly available in most grocery stores and International aisle of most super markets. Also, available in most local Asian markets.

Lemongrass - is a type of tropical island plant in the grass family and used widely in many tropical regions. It's very common in the Thai and Vietnamese cuisines. Is available in some grocery stores and International aisle of some super markets. Also, available in most local Asian markets.

Oyster Sauce - Bottled oyster-flavored sauce is a rich, concentrated mixture of oyster extractives, soy sauce, brine, and assorted seasonings. The brown sauce is thick, salty, and strong. It is used sparingly to enhance the flavor of many dishes that have a long list of additional wet and aromatic ingredients. Is wildly available in most grocery stores and International aisle of most super markets. Also, available in most local Asian markets.

Plantains - are a member of the banana family. They are a starchy, low in sugar variety that is cooked before serving. Unlike bananas, plantains are typically cooked before eating. It is used in many savory dishes somewhat like a potato would be used and is very popular in Western Africa and the Caribbean countries. Is available in some grocery stores and in the produce section near bananas. Also, available in most local Spanish markets.

Red Miso - This is typically made from soybeans fermented with barley or other grains, though with a higher percentage of soybeans and/or a longer fermentation period. The deep umami flavor of red miso can overwhelm mild dishes, but is perfect for hearty soups, braises, and glazes. Is available in some grocery stores and International aisle of some super markets. Also, available in most local Asian markets.

Rice Noodles - Made from white rice flour, rice noodles are most commonly sold dried. Is wildly available in most grocery stores and International aisle of most super markets. Also, available in most local Asian markets.

Rice Wine - also known as mijiu, is an alcoholic drink made from rice, traditionally consumed in East Asia, Southeast Asia, and South Asia. Rice wine is made from the fermentation of rice starch that has been converted to sugars. Is wildly available in most grocery stores where cooking wines are located and International aisle of most super markets. Also, available in most local Asian markets.

Serrano Pepper - originated in the Mexican states of Puebla and Hidalgo. Serrano peppers are perfect for salsas, sauces, relishes, garnishes, and more. The serrano pepper is similar to the jalapeño in its look, but this pepper is much hotter. On the Scoville heat index, the serrano pepper can be between 10,000 and 25,000. This pepper is usually small (around 2 inches) and green in color. As a rule of thumb, the smaller the serrano pepper, the hotter it will taste. Serrano peppers are usually right with all the other peppers -- jalapenos, etc.

Shirataki Noodles - are thin, translucent, gelatinous traditional Japanese noodles made from the konjac yam (devil's tongue yam or elephant yam). The word "shirataki" means "white waterfall", describing the appearance of these noodles. Largely composed of water and glucomannan, a water-soluble dietary fiber, they are very low in digestible carbohydrates and calories, and have little flavor of their own. Is available in most grocery stores and International aisle of most super markets. Also, available in most local Asian markets.

Shrimp Paste - is a common ingredient used in Southeast Asian and Southern Chinese cuisine. It is made from fermented ground shrimp or krill mixed with salt. It is an essential ingredient in many curries and sauces. Shrimp paste can be found in most meals in Indonesia, Laos, Malaysia, Myanmar, Singapore, Thailand, Vietnam, and the Philippines. It is often an ingredient in dip for fish or vegetables. Is available in some grocery stores and International aisle of some super markets. Also, available in most local Asian markets.

Tamarind Soup Mix - is the "secret ingredient" in a lot of Asian cooking. A combination of sweet and sour, it just gives some dishes an extra "oomph" that they wouldn't have otherwise. Tamarind soup base or mix comes in a packet. Knorr is a very popular brand of soup mixes. Is available in some grocery stores and International aisle of some super markets or where packaged soup mixes are sold, like Knorr. Also, available in most local Asian markets.

Thai Chili Peppers - Theses peppers now featuring in the sauce known around the world as Sriracha are red Serrano. When they are fully mature, they turn red. On the Scoville heat scale units: 50,000 – 100,000. Forty times hotter than a Jalapeño. Is available in some grocery stores and in the produce section usually right with all the other peppers -- jalapenos, etc. Also, available in most local Asian markets.

Watercress - is a dark, leafy green grown in natural spring water. An ancient green plant said to have been a staple in the diet of Roman soldiers. Watercress is a part of the cruciferous (also known as brassica) family of vegetables along with kale, broccoli, arugula, and Brussels sprouts. Is wildly available in most grocery stores where other green leafy vegetables are sold. Also, available in most local Asian markets.

Index

Thank You

Before you go, I'd like to say thank you for purchasing my Book. I know you have a lot of options online for cookbooks.
So, a big thank you!

If you like this book, please take a moment to leave a review for this book. It really does make a difference.

If you want to keep you up to date for new recipes, cookbooks, and posts, follow me on Social Media.

Follow Kevin on Facebook: www.facebook.com/kmcordeiro
Twitter: www.twitter.com/kevinmarkc
Instagram: www.instagram.com/homechefkevin
Pinterest: www.pinterest.com/kevinskitchen
Web Page: www.kevinshomecooking.com

Thank you once again for your business.
Yours sincerely,
Kevin M. Cordeiro

Made in the USA
Middletown, DE
23 December 2017